SOCIAL MEDIA
OVERLOAD

SIMPLE SOCIAL MEDIA STRATEGIES
FOR OVERWHELMED AND
TIME-DEPRIVED BUSINESSES

COREY PERLMAN

SOCIAL MEDIA OVERLOAD!

SIMPLE SOCIAL MEDIA STRATEGIES
FOR OVERWHELMED AND
TIME-DEPRIVED BUSINESSES

AUTHOR OF
EBOOT
CAMP!

COREY PERLMAN

Coweta Public Library System
85 Literary Lane
Newnan, GA 30265
770-683-2052
www.cowetapubliclibrary.org

Copyright © 2014 by Corey Perlman

Published by
Garnet Group Publishing
Roswell, GA

All rights reserved. No part of this book may be reproduced or transmitted in any form or by any means, electronic or mechanical, including photocopying, recording, or by any information retrieval or storage system, without the prior written consent of the publisher.

ISBN: 978-0-9915404-0-2
First Printing
Printed in the United States of America

Interior Design by GKS Creative
The cover image created by Primate for 8 Gram Gorilla
primate.co.uk | 8gramgorilla.com

Publisher's Cataloging-in-Publication
Perlman, Corey, 1978-
    Social media overload : simple social media
strategies for overwhelmed and time-deprived businesses
/ Corey Perlman.
    pages cm
    ISBN 978-0-9915404-0-2

    1. Internet marketing--Social aspects. 2. Social
media--Economic aspects.   I. Title.

HF5415.1265.P47 2014   659.14'4
                    QBI14-600055

I dedicate this book to my mom; you are the guiding light from above that continuously directs me toward serving others.

To my wife; my partner in love, life and laughter.

And to you, Dad, thank you for being a beautiful example of what it is to be a man, a father, and an entrepreneur.

Advance Praise

Corey Perlman is a thought leader and go-to resource in the social media space. This book offers executives and their staff a roadmap to a simple and successful social media strategy. I've benefited from his insights and so will you.

Mark Sanborn
President of Sanborn & Associates, Inc.
Bestselling author of *The Fred Factor* and *Fred 2.0*

Perlman's first book was the catalyst behind kick-starting an amazing online journey that has not only brought me more customers, but also launched a personal brand, speaking career, an info-product business, a book deal, and more opportunities than I can shake a stick at! **Social Media Overload** *is now going to help me take it all to a whole new level!*

Chris Ducker
Author of *Virtual Freedom: How to Work with Virtual Staff to Buy More Time, Become More Productive, and Build Your Dream Business*

Corey Perlman provides a rich resource in **Social Media Overload** *for a Social-weary-but-love-it-still world. We love social media, but how do we allocate our time and resources? He gives several serious, step-by-step ideas for businesses on how to deal with it without going to either extreme (nothing at all or constantly-consumed). This is a good book that goes way beyond the now widely known ("Only 140 characters in Twitter") to the imminently-useful and desperately-needed. Get this book. Read it. Study it. Profit from it.*

Terry L. Brock, MBA, CSP, CPAE
Speaker Hall of Fame, Syndicated Columnist with Business Journals,
Past Editor-in-Chief for AT&T's largest business blog,
Past Chief Enterprise Blogger for Skype, all-around nice guy

This book is a perfect guide for helping our dealers sell more bikes on the web.

Christy LaCurelle
Marketing Manager, KTM North America

Social Media Overload is a must read for business owners and corporate executive teams looking to produce meaningful content that connects and converts. It will help you cut through the clutter and finally see business results!

Heather Lutze
Bestselling Author and Internet Marketing Expert, (Findability.com)

In his second book, Social Media Overload, Corey has once again taken the complex and made it simple. Amen! With everyone trying to do more with less, social media can at times feel like a huge time suck and hassle. While it is a non-negotiable to ignore social media, finding the time to make social media a part of your marketing is the real challenge. This book and proven advice will save you a ton of time and stress on the path to making social media work for you, not against you. Thank you again Corey for sharing your wisdom at a time when millions of businesses and non-profits are struggling to find help on the social media highway when it comes to understanding and effectively employing it now and into the future!

Tony Rubleski
Chief Agent of Positive Change, MindCaptureGroup.com

"This info works! We've implemented the digital marketing strategies from this book and had one of our best year's ever! Up 32%!"

John Covert
Dale Carnegie Franchisee

"Corey teaches digital strategies that deliver results. We can directly attribute over $100,000 in business in our first year of working with Corey and his team."

David MacAngus
MacAngus & Associates, Ltd.

TABLE OF CONTENTS

ACKNOWLEDGMENTS

"No member of a crew is praised for the rugged individuality of his rowing." –Ralph Waldo Emerson

My boat was filled with a team of amazing rowers and I'd like to acknowledge some of them here.

I'd like to start with the amazing people I get to call my clients…and my friends. It is with you that the strategies in this book have been tried and proven. Thank you for the trust and faith you put in our team. We will continue to work tirelessly for you, your employees, and your families.

Thank you to my tremendous eBoot Camp team - Jodi Alcock (The engine), Jess Nicklos, Natalie Palacios, Hazel Zanoria, and PJ Edrozo.

I want to thank Bethany Brown of the Cadence Group for being my all-star quarterback on this project. You made this a smooth and enjoyable process and I can't wait to work with you again.

Thank you to GKS Creative for taking a boring manuscript and transforming it into this beautiful book.

Thank you to John Marcus, Julie Cotant, Jessica Pettitt, Maria Dawson Torsney, Jeremy and Tara Overton for crossing all of my t's and dotting all my i's. I'm so lucky to be surrounded by your brilliant minds!

A book can do little good if it never gets in the hands of others. Thank you to Amy Collins of New Shelves Book Distribution for your efforts in getting the book to the masses. I'm lucky to have found you.

I want to thank my all-star team of guest authors: Jay Baer, Terry Brock, Heather Lutze, David Newman, Michael Tigue, and Erik Qualman.

A special thank you to Joe Hart for your constant encouragement, support, and loving faith.

Oh, where would I be without my family? I love you Jess, Talia, Milo, Dad, Kate, Jaime, Mom and Dad Duke, Jon, and Liz!

SECTION ONE

AIM BEFORE YOU FIRE

You don't have to **be on Twitter.**

I said that once in front of 500 dentists and they immediately stood up and started cheering. I had no idea it had gotten that bad.

But it was a gentleman from another event who shed light on just how serious this problem had become. He walked up to me before I took the stage and said,

"Corey, I really need to work on getting my Twitter feed syndicated on my website. Will you be covering that?"

"I won't be covering that today, but come up after and I'll help," I replied.

Before he sat down, I asked him why he wanted to get his Twitter feed on his website. His answer:

"Because I saw it on one of my competitor's sites."

"Well, who's your target demographic?" I asked.

"I deal with medical benefits for retirees, so my customer is 55 years and older…"

There was an awkward silence of about 20 seconds where we just stared at each other. You could almost see the light bulb pop on.

He said "My customers aren't really on Twitter, are they?" I shook my head no.

"Then why bother?" he asked.

"You don't," I replied.

You don't need to be on every social media site. I repeat: you don't need to be on every social media site.

Facebook, LinkedIn, Twitter, Foursquare, Pinterest, oh my! Overwhelmed yet? No? Don't forget Tumblr, Instagram and did you know MySpace is primed for a comeback? How's your stress level now? You have two choices when it comes to your social media strategy:

Focus on a few and excel, or be a Jack of all social media sites—master of none.

You need to decide which digital strategies are right for your business. And cut out the rest.

Before you even think about your Facebook page or email marketing schedule, you need to take a step back and figure out where your prospects and customers are hanging out online. Then you can prioritize the areas on the web where you will focus your time and resources. This is the step that is almost always skipped and is the reason why so many businesses struggle to see results with their digital marketing efforts.

Once you have determined the sites that you are going to focus on, then you have to develop your digital marketing plan. You have one of those, right? This is the guide that every person who ever touches your website, blog, LinkedIn page, or any other digital asset must have in front of them. Every tweet you send out and every video you upload to YouTube has a purpose in your overall digital marketing plan.

You will never tweet just for the sake of tweeting ever again. (Note: This is also a rule in my house but takes on an entirely different meaning.)

You have some work to do prior to diving into a specific strategy or tool. But trust that this work will be the difference between seeing actual results from your efforts or simply spinning your virtual wheels.

Best Practice:

In every private consultation I have with a company, we start by answering some basic questions that help steer the remainder of our conversation. It gets them thinking about the overall strategy prior to heading down a particular path.

What are you trying to accomplish: brand awareness, new leads, customer engagement, etc.? Consider the following:

1. What's your content strategy: to entertain, to inform, to solicit feedback, etc.?
2. Who will execute your plan: an intern, an outside firm, your team, etc.?
3. How will you measure results: web traffic, web leads, sales, engagement, etc.?

This is a start, but a good plan should be reviewed and updated on a consistent basis. The more the executive team is involved in the big picture, the better your chance for success.

FAQ: If our audience is not 55 years or older, will you tell us how to syndicate our Twitter feed to our website?

A. You really missed the point of that story.

B. For those of you who read *eBoot Camp!*, you know it was very tactical with a lot of "how to" information. This book will be a bit different. Less tactical, more strategic. Sometimes, I can't help myself and I will offer some of my favorite social media strategies that generate results. But in general, I plan to stay above the minutiae and offer more fundamentals that won't change by the time this book goes to print. My goal is for you to find as much value from the book five years from now as you do today.

FISH WHERE THE FISH ARE

So, HOW DO YOU decide which social media sites to focus on? You must first figure out where your prospects and customers are hanging out online. You can get this information by sending out an email survey, having your employees ask at checkout if you're a retail outlet, or simply by having some informal conversations with clients. You will eventually get to a consensus about where they spend the majority of their web time. Ask them where they have profiles and—this is key—how they interact with those sites. They might have a Pinterest account but only visit it once a month. Or they may be very active on Facebook but only in the evenings after work. This is all helpful information on how you will develop your digital marketing strategy.

*Note: You might notice I tend to use the phrase **Digital Marketing** instead of **Social Media**. Social media is the common buzz phrase, but it tends to leave out important areas for your overall web strategy. I believe online assets, such as your website, blog, and email newsletters, are equally important parts of your overall digital marketing strategy; those assets don't fall under the category of social media. Social media is a conversation, while digital marketing tends to be more one-sided.*

Another way of finding out where your customers and prospects are hanging out online is by checking your web analytics. Analytics will tell you which sites are referring the most traffic to your website. I use Google Analytics for this—it's free and easy to install on your site. If you've spent equal time promoting on Facebook and Twitter thus far, and one is at the top of your referring sites and the other isn't on the list, that tells you one is more effective than the other.

You also can follow industry reports. Sites like Comscore.com love to share data about people and companies and how often they frequent social media sites. Do some searching and you can find out some very specific data about your industry and its online activity. We have to aim before we fire.

Best Practice:
I recently did a private consultation with a commercial construction company. During our time together, I asked them to fill out a graph similar to the one below. We placed different web activities on the graph based on how frequently or infrequently they believed their customers and prospects participated in that activity.

As a group, we began to make assumptions about where their customers and prospects were spending time online. I challenged them to put some data behind this by either surveying their clients or doing some general research online. We were one step closer to figuring out the right places for this company to focus its time and attention.

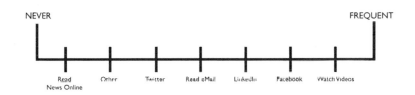

Now, it's your turn! Here's a blank graph for you to fill out based on how you think your customers and prospects are spending time online. Consider the activities listed below the graph as you fill it in.

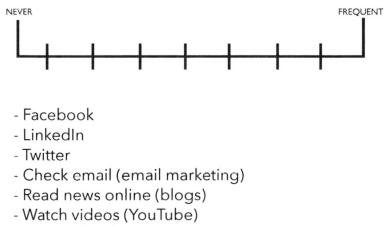

- Facebook
- LinkedIn
- Twitter
- Check email (email marketing)
- Read news online (blogs)
- Watch videos (YouTube)
- Other (an activity I didn't think of?)

CREATE YOUR SOCIAL MEDIA SALES FUNNEL

GENERATE LEADS	Facebook Advertising, Google Advertising, Search Engine Optimization (SEO)
BUILD CREDIBILITY	Website, Local Directories, Social Media Profiles
STAY TOP OF MIND	Social Media Postings, E-mail Marketing, Blog
DRIVE TO SWEET SPOT	Specials, Exclusive Offers, Discounts, Clear Call to Action
STRENGTHEN RELATIONSHIP	Personal Facebook Page, LinkedIn Profile
EARN REFERRALS	Online Testimonials, Reviews, Get Introduced, Feature on LinkedIn

I'M FULLY AWARE THAT looking at social media through a sales lens can be a recipe for disaster if taken too literally, but the opposite can be true as well. By concentrating so much on conversation and content, you can end up tossing social media into the proverbial "waste of time" pile. If you're using social media for business, then you must have a process for taking people from prospect to customer. As I do in most of the chapters in the book, I'm simply pulling back the curtain on our social media agency and showing you what we do for ourselves and our clients. Therefore, the image above is the social media funnel all our clients are encouraged to follow, and I will go into detail about how my business uses each category.

At the top of the funnel is **Generating Leads**. This is where people find out about our business for the first time. This category comprises most of the digital advertising strategies that we use. This is also where many companies start (and end!) when looking for social media results. This is unfortunate because many of the strategies we discuss can go way beyond just generating leads. If you only focus on a single category, you might be setting yourself up for disappointment. Below are some of the additional results we look for when implementing a digital marketing strategy.

Staying "Top of Mind" (consistently staying on a customer or prospect's mind) is a critical step in the process. Often, people are in research mode and not ready to buy. They may learn about us in January, but may not be ready to buy from us until September. Many of the strategies outlined in this book will help you stay Top of Mind from the moment prospects meet you until they become a customer.

In most cases, we will never close a sale on a social media site. Believing we can close sales via social media is a big misconception and is often why businesses don't see results from their social media marketing. Instead, we should **Drive People to Our Sweet Spot**—the place where we typically close business. So if you're a kitchen remodeling company, your sweet spot is either in your showroom or in the prospect's home. If you're a car salesman, your sweet spot is in that beautiful car during a test drive!

Your funnel should always lead to your sweet spot.

The last two sections of your funnel are where you can harness the true power of social media. The first is by **Strengthening Relationships**. The old adage that "it's easier to keep a customer than to gain a new one" still holds true today, and social media provides a powerful way to build deeper relationships with your customers. This step will not be in every sales funnel, but for those with longstanding clients, this is one you should take very seriously.

The final section of the funnel is **Earning Referrals**. Why waste time cold-calling when your best customers can be your sales force? If you really boil it down, social media is word-of-mouth on steroids. If you can offer platforms for your customers to tell the world why they love you, then they just might become your greatest sales force.

There you have it. Almost every client we have follows this model for their digital marketing strategy. We work in many different industries so there's always room for customization, but this funnel is always the foundation. Think of it as the flux capacitor of this book. And if you don't know what a flux capacitor is, you need to catch up on your awesome 1980s movies!

The next step is to determine which individual digital marketing tools you should use for each section of the funnel. This is where you can begin to decide which tools to focus on and which to leave behind.

SECTION TWO

GENERATE LEADS

LEADS ARE THE LIFEBLOOD of any business, and the web has become the go-to place for advertisers. It has leveled the playing field and allowed mom-and-pop shops to compete with the largest companies in the world. Because there are so many places on the web to compete for traffic, businesses have to be strategic about where they focus their time and money.

As previously discussed, the first step is figuring out where your prospects are spending time online, then planting yourself on those sites to capture their attention. The challenge with any lead-generation strategy is the ability to hit your target market. As the battle of social media and search engine supremacy continues, a key factor in determining a winner will be the one who can pull the most data from its users. The more these sites can learn about their users, the more valuable they become to marketers and advertisers.

Facebook and Google have been the clear winners in this area thus far. There are others in the race, such as LinkedIn, YouTube, Pinterest, and Pandora, but they are still far behind the big two. Google is still the behemoth in the search game and as long as people keep searching for products and services on its site, we will continue to advertise on it as a strategy for our clients.

The reason Facebook is so compelling to businesses is the sheer amount of data it has on its users. Facebook knows where we live, where we work, our age, our likes, dislikes, and so much more. It is, by far, the most targeted advertising strategy I know of and the most competitive.

The following chapters are some of my favorite ways to generate new leads for your business. Over time, these sites may change, but the rules will remain the same. Digital advertising is all about positioning yourself in the places where your prospects are spending the most time.

3

ADVERTISING ON GOOGLE AND FACEBOOK

ADVERTISING ON GOOGLE AND Facebook is all about paying to play. Here, we're not trying to engage in conversation or add value. We're just trying to be above our competition when prospects are in research or buy mode.

In most industries, consumers often begin their buying process on a search engine. According to Comscore.com, the vast majority of search traffic still occurs on Google, where more than 60 percent of total searches are conducted. Because Google still has a stronghold on the search market share, we tend to focus most of our search budget on Google. That said, for some clients, we spend a small portion of our ad budget with other search engines such as Bing.com.

As a quick review, the image below depicts exactly where Google allows businesses to pay for placement.

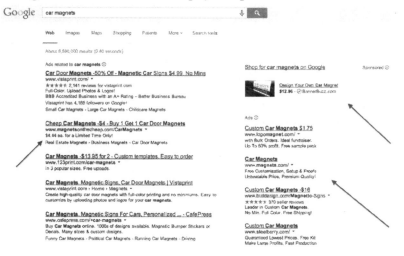

FAQ: What words should I pay Google to rank?

When we manage an ad campaign on Google, we look for phrases where our client's website is not found in the top five search results. If it's an important search phrase, we get them ranking with a paid ad. We can then spend some time working on getting them to rank better organically (the non-paid results listed below or to the left of the ads), but at least they are showing up at the top until we do.

Case Study

One of our clients owns a bathroom remodeling business. He ranks very well organically in certain cities within his service area, but he also ranks poorly in a few of the outlying areas. We will buy ads on Google for those outlying areas because, even though his business services those areas, it's tougher to rank organically.

FAQ: How much should I budget for Google ads?

That depends on how competitive the phrases are for which you're trying to rank. We only do cost-per-click (CPC) campaigns, which can vary from less than $1 to $7 or more.

Case Study

Another client, a video production company, is located in Ferndale, Michigan, but travels all over the metro Detroit area. When people searched "Video Production Detroit," the company had a tough time ranking organically in a very competitive space. Then, the client started to pay to rank for that phrase along with a few others. The company immediately saw an increase in leads, which directly increased business. One customer actually told our client that he decided to work with them because they advertised on Google. He felt that because the company invested in advertising, it legitimized it as a business and made him feel more comfortable working with them.

Facebook Advertising

We also like advertising on Facebook because of its powerful targeting opportunities. We can narrow our target market by factors including but not limited to:

- Age
- Sex
- Education level
- Interests
- Relationship status, and more

We have one client whose primary buyers are women age 55 and older. We are able to limit our ads only to profiles that meet that exact criteria. There are not many advertising options that are capable of such targeting.

And with the revolution of smartphones in full swing, savvy marketers are taking advantage of being early adopters of both Facebook and Google mobile advertising. According to *The Wall Street Journal*, as of October 2013, people are spending more than two hours a day on their phones doing things other than talking, so there's a huge opportunity to get our ads seen during their time on Facebook or Google.

Best Practice: Promoted Posts

If you post something on your Facebook business page, on average, Facebook only shows that post to about 20 percent of your fans. Yes, feel free to reread that last sentence and let it sink in. Why are they doing this? Well, how many of you have actually paid money to Facebook? Not a lot, and that's an issue for Facebook and its stockholders. Facebook addresses this issue by asking us to pay to have our post seen by more of our fans. This form of Facebook advertising is called "promoted posts." We can pay to have our messages seen by more of our fans and, if we want, friends of our fans.

Is this fair? Maybe not. However, if we're going to play on Facebook's field, we have to play by their rules. The days of free ads are over. Just ask Mark Cuban, owner of the Dallas Mavericks. He uses the Mavericks' Facebook fan page to connect with Mavs fans and offer discounted tickets. When promoted posts were launched, Facebook required Mark to pay around $3,000 per post to get his message out to all of his fans. Mark was outraged and threatened to leave Facebook for...of all sites...MySpace! As of this writing, he's still playing by Facebook's rules.

If you're not a fan of the traditional Facebook ads that show up on the right side of the page, then you might consider using promoted posts instead. These show up inside the news feed of Facebook users. Let's say you have a new product or an event coming up and you want to advertise it on Facebook. You can post it on your Facebook page, pay a bit of money, then display it in the same place as all the other messages your fans see.

This is how Facebook explains the process: "Your promoted post will be seen by a larger percentage of people who liked your page than would normally see it and would also show it to friends of people who interact with your post."

FAQ: How much do these promoted posts cost?

Facebook will offer you a range based on how many fans and friends of fans you'd like to reach with your message. So, it can range from as little as $5.00 per post to as much as a few hundred dollars for pages with larger audiences.

FAQ: What types of posts should I promote?

To get the biggest bang for your buck, try to only promote posts that can get you a return on your investment. A good example would be an invite to an open house or an event where you can potentially make some sales. We also had clients promote job openings at their companies. An example of a post that probably would not warrant spending money on would be a "happy birthday" wish to one of your employees or a "good luck" post to your local sports teams.

Case Study

One of our clients recently held an open house, so we advertised the event through a series of promoted posts. We spent less than $100 and were able to get information out to about 500 of their Facebook fans and another couple hundred of their friends. We offered a free gift to those who mentioned Facebook. This allowed us to track the number of attendees that came as a result of our Facebook marketing campaign, which turned out to be half of our total attendees.

4

GET FOUND ORGANICALLY

LET'S GO BACK TO the importance of appearing at the top of the page in Google searches. This chapter will offer some opportunities to show up organically and get new prospects into your sales funnel.

Obviously, we all want our business's website to rank first in a search. For those of you who read my first book, *eBoot Camp!*, you know I wrote a lot about ways to get your website to rank higher on the search engines. Many things have changed since then, but some of the fundamentals are still the same.

You should still have:

- A quality title tag for every page on your site.
- Good content on each of your web pages that includes critical keywords. Keywords are words entered in search engines in order to find a product or service like yours. If you're an accountant in Seattle, some critical keywords for you would be "Accountant Seattle WA."
- Inbound links from other reputable, relevant sites.

Some new SEO (Search Engine Optimization) factors that you should include:

- Fresh content. Having a blog on your website offers the opportunity for fresh content on a consistent basis. In Chapter Eleven, I will discuss blogs and how to write effective blog articles.
- Make your site social. Get those social media plugins on your site and allow others to Like, +1 you, and more. The more others are noticing your site, the more the search engines will notice your site.

Make sure to **read our guest chapter** by Heather Lutze (Chapter Twenty-Four) on how to boost your rankings using social search!

Some things you don't have to worry about as much:

- Reciprocal links. It's better to get one-way links straight to your site than do a mutual link exchange. Google and other search engines tend to discount reciprocal link exchanges.

- Meta keywords. These are the words that you add behind the scenes on your site. I still think it's good to have them, but don't waste too much time worrying about getting them exactly right. Most search engines pay attention to the words on the front side of your website that are visible to everyone.

- Description tag. This once represented the black text that showed up under the blue link when your site would rank on Google (see image below). These days, Google tends to show content from the front side of your site for this area instead of the description tag from the backside of your site. My advice is to include a description tag but have similar content on the front side as well. This way, you will guarantee that you like what you see on Google and other search engines.

Arthur Murray Dance Studio
www.sacramentodancesport.com/ ▾
The Arthur Murray® Sacramento dance instructors are specially trained and certified in the many forms of ballroom dancing. Our dance instructors can put you in ...

Studio T Urban Dance Academy | Sacramento Dance, Sacr...
www.studiotdance.com/ ▾
Studio T Urban Dance Academy is a dance studio in Sacramento, CA providing hip hop dance lessons and dance classes of all styles to all ages. Located at ...

SACRAMENTO & DAVIS POLE DANCE STUDIO
www.sacramentopoledancestudio.com/ ▾
Sacramento Pole Dance Studio - Beautiful, Sexy, and Confident. An alternative to regular exersise. Sacramento's hottest new pole dance studio. Formerly known ...

Dance Studios in Sacramento, CA on Yahoo Local
local.yahoo.com › ... › Entertainment & Arts › Dance ▾ Yahoo! Local ▾
Results 1 - 10 of 36 - Dance Studios in Sacramento, CA on Yahoo Local Get ...

4	Step One Sacramento Dance	(916) 448-7837	1920 T St
6	Sacramento Academy of Dance	(916) 971-0945	2818 Marconi Ave

The boxed content either comes from your description tag or the first sentence on your website. As I mentioned, be sure Google picks up the content you want by making your description tag and first sentence on the page be the same thing.

There are other ways beyond maintaining your website to have a presence at the top of search engines. If you have a physical location, having a Google+ Local business page is essential if you want a high Google ranking when people search geographically (for example, "chiropractor Royal Oak, Michigan").

In the example above, the boxed results are Google+ Local business pages, which rank right below paid ads and a few major directories. You'll find more information on Google+ Local Business coming up in Chapter Seven.

Take Action!

Claim your listing and create a robust profile with quality content, images, and even video! Because these pages change so often, adding instructions here would be futile. Instead, feel free to visit www.SocialMediaOverload.com for a video with specific instructions on how to claim your page and enter all of your critical info.

You also should establish listings on any other directory that ranks in important geographical searches. For example, let's say you're an accountant in Miami. Do a Google search for "accountant Miami, Florida" and see which directories appear on the first page. If you see Yelp, then establish a presence on Yelp.com. If Accountants Directory of the World (I made that up) does not show up anywhere on the first or even second page, you may consider ignoring that directory.

*Note: Yes, I recognize that Google is not the only search engine out there, and I'm sure there are directories that don't rank on Google but still drive lots of leads to local businesses. This book is all about **efficiency and prioritization**. I want you to focus on the dominant search engine and the dominant directories. When you have a firm grasp on those, you can begin to entertain other engines and directories.*

Some other ways to rank organically on search engines:

Videos. Remember, YouTube is owned by Google and YouTube videos often get good Google juice for many searches. If you're a real estate agent, consider posting a YouTube video of a virtual house tour and title it with words that potential homebuyers might use on Google.

Also, don't forget to check out Chapter Twenty on YouTube, written by guest author, Erik Qualman, later in the book!

Images. Sites like Pinterest and Instagram are great places to place your images. When titled well, these images can show up high in a Google search. Try any search with a person's name, and if he or she has a photo on the web, that will often be the first thing to show up.

Social Media. Sites like Facebook, LinkedIn, and Twitter get great Google juice for your brand names. Search for *eBoot Camp,* and you'll see that our company profiles all rank on page one. You obviously want your branded searches to be filled up with sites you manage, so make sure to have those profiles created and updated.

Case Study

One of the quickest private consultations I ever had was with a dentist in Michigan. He ranked fairly high for "dentist" but was nowhere to be found if you searched "dental implants." This was a challenge for him, since performing dental implants was one of his primary services. I suggested two fixes that made quite a difference. We created a page within his website dedicated to dental implants. We titled the page with those keywords and used them in prominent places throughout the page. I also noticed that he did not have dental implants listed as one of his categories in his Google+ Local business page. We simply added that service to his categories and clicked update.

Both of these improvements resulted in page-one placement for his business when the keywords "dental implants" in his geographical area were entered. It's not always this easy, but there are often simple fixes like this that can make a big impact on your search engine ranking.

FAQ: I'm not sure I fully understand "title tags."
Can you explain that again?

Your title tag is the most important sentence you will ever create on the web.

I have been talking about title tags for almost 10 years, and it's one of the few principles of search engine optimization that has remained relatively unchanged. Yet, in each city I visit, most crowds are still unfamiliar with what they are and why they are important.

When you show up on a search engine, the blue link that is displayed is typically taken from your title tag.

Search engines do not like to guess; they ask you for a title tag and you give it to them by putting it on your website. If you're strategic about what your title tag is, and you place it correctly on your website, Google will almost always use it in their search engine.

Appropriate title tags are essential. When someone does a search on a search engine, he or she typically makes a decision based on a quick scan of those blue links (see example below). That person then decides which result is most likely going to give him or her the most relevant information. If your title tag is too long or too vague, they'll probably skip over you and head straight to your competition.

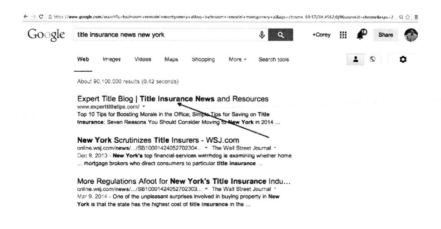

Of course, the above situation assumes that you actually appear in a searcher's results. Your title tag is still a key indicator as to whether you rank for a particular search phrase. Go conduct a few searches of your own on Google. Scan the title tags that come up on page one and notice that Google puts the words in the title tags that you used in your search in bold lettering. It's not a coincidence that every result has at least a few of your search words in each title tag.

So, use keywords in your title tag.

You also want to be careful not to get the infamous "...". No matter how big or small you are, you still only get about seven or eight words before the search engines cut you off. Look at this example:

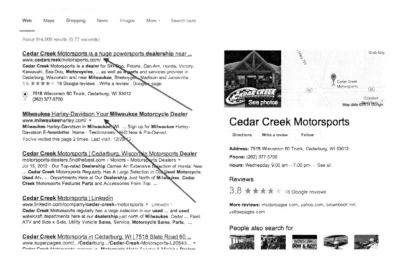

The first example seems to be cut off before some of its critical information is displayed. This occurs in a really unfortunate place. All that this business needs to do is to shorten its title tag a bit, and the issue should be fixed. The next result down is a better example of getting all the critical information in with fewer words.

If you're interested in knowing where to find your title tag, it typically shows up at the top of your browser. If you don't see it there, you can also check the source code behind your site.

A good title tag should include the name of your business and a very descriptive tagline that leaves no doubt about what you do. If you're a local business, then I highly suggest you include your geographical location in your title tag.

5

ATTEND ONLINE NETWORKING GROUPS

JUST LIKE IN THE offline world, sometimes you have to get out there and kiss some hands and shake some babies. No, wait…that doesn't sound right.

Anyway, my favorite online place to do this is in LinkedIn groups. It's a super-efficient way to interact with people who have interests similar to yours. Maybe you live in the same area, went to the same school, or work in the same industry. With just a few minutes of searching on LinkedIn, you can join some groups where you can be both a valuable resource and a contributor.

Have you ever walked up to someone at a networking event and had the person jump right into a sales pitch before you had the chance to finish your cucumber and salmon crostini? It's not cool in the offline world, and the same rules apply online.

You join these groups to interact and offer value. Business is generated organically as you get to know people better and they get to know you and learn about the products or services you offer. Go in looking to help people, and you won't risk being the cheesy sales guy or gal who gets booted out of the group.

FAQ: How do you decide when a group is not for you?

When you stop receiving value from it. Often, groups become spammy because they are not monitored properly. You should remove yourself from these groups so you can concentrate on the groups that will give you value. I have probably joined hundreds of groups over the years, but I'm an active member on only about ten. These groups are huge resources for me and my business.

FAQ: This is in the lead-generation section. Yet, you're telling us not to sell our products and services. What gives?

Feisty today, aren't we? You are right; it does sound a bit counterintuitive. When you join a LinkedIn group, you enter an arena with people you don't know who could use your products or services. The challenge is being able to sell to them without coming off as "that guy" or "that gal." A good way to start is by finding ways to add value to the group. Try to become a valued member that people get used to and enjoy hearing from. Over time, people will ask questions or make comments that will offer an opportunity for you to potentially work with them. I would try to take that conversation offline, where it might be more appropriate to discuss your products or services. Send them a private message on LinkedIn, suggest a phone call, or offer to meet with them at a location of their choosing. Once out of the group conversation, you can feel a little more comfortable being in sales mode and seeing if it makes sense to do business together.

Best Practice: Get the Most out of Your LinkedIn Group Experience

My friend Ryan Jenkins, a fellow keynote speaker, has had tremendous success with LinkedIn groups. The following is an excerpt from a guest blog post he did for eBoot Camp on LinkedIn Groups:

> I post to my blog twice a week, and if any of my content is applicable to a particular group, I will post a link to the blog along with a thought-provoking discussion question.
>
> I usually get a few likes or comments per discussion post. However, I posted my article "What Everybody Ought To Know About...The Myth Of Experience" into the "Future Trends" LinkedIn group and, in just a few weeks, it's generated thirty-two likes and ninety-eight-plus comments. The next closest article in the group has only thirty-nine comments.
>
> I do not share these stats to impress you but rather to impress upon you how valuable LinkedIn groups can be for your brand or business.

Here are seven ways to get the most out of your LinkedIn group experience:

Value-Added Content. The content that you share must bring value to your intended audience. If the content falls flat, you're sunk. Nothing else will matter.

Catchy Title. Ensure the title of your discussion is succinct and attention grabbing. My title was: "Is experience irrelevant these days?" If you choose to add additional details, use it to create more interest. I used: "Before you answer that...consider these trends."

Relevant Content. The content shared must relate to the theme of the group. For example, do not post "How to Perfect Your Golf Swing" in the Future Trends group.

Concise Content. You will capture more readers if your content is scan-able, scrollable, and skim-able. Stay clear of long or heavy content. Shoot for fewer than 500 words.

Engaging Picture. Use the "attach a link" function when posting a discussion. This will add the picture associated with your article. In addition, ensure that your profile picture is inviting and that it communicates you are a pleasant person. A close-up shot of your smiling face is ideal. Remember, these two pictures are like the billboard of your discussion.

Controversial. Content that takes a stance and goes against the grain is naturally going to stir up more conversation. The haters will hate (just check out some of the comments I got on my discussion). Don't be afraid to be contrarian, but do not tolerate malicious comments. Continually encourage people to keep the discussion constructive and productive.

Established Group. Make sure the groups you contribute to are active and have a large enough audience to make it worth your time. As a reference, Future Trends has 229,000 members and multiple discussions are posted every day.

Leverage these must-haves and you will find how truly rewarding it can be when you serve up valuable content that stretches the thinking of the group and creates productive discussion. Create your epic content and go grow your audience via LinkedIn groups. To learn more about Ryan, visit his website at www.ryan-jenkins.com.

SECTION THREE

BUILD CREDIBILITY

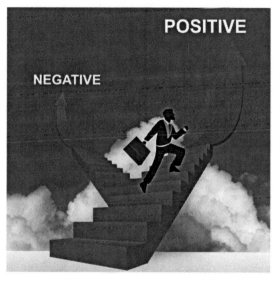

NO MATTER HOW GREAT our products and services are, we still lose business to our competition from time to time. The sad thing is that we rarely find out why. No one ever calls us up and says, "Yeah, I was going to do business with you, but then I went to your website, and it was confusing and crowded, so I went someplace else." They just go somewhere else and take their money with them. More than ever before, people are making buying decisions online instead of face-to-face or over the phone. It is our job to give off the best impression we can and to give people every reason to buy from us and not from our competition.

There are three digital profiles people commonly consider when making a buying decision, and those areas are discussed in our next three chapters.

- Website
- Google+
- LinkedIn Profile

This is a critical step that often gets overlooked in digital marketing strategies. You can have the greatest products or services on the planet, but still lose customers on a daily basis due to an issue with your web presence.

I think the hardest part is generating the quality leads, although this should be the easiest. More often than not, this is where businesses drop the ball. **It's the number one mistake I see businesses make.**

The question you must ask yourself is: do I have as strong a presence online as I do offline?

6

IF YOUR WEBSITE SUCKS, SOCIAL MEDIA CAN'T HELP YOU

THIS PAST YEAR, I delivered a keynote presentation to 200 motorcycle dealers in Northern California. The hotel was decked out with the coolest bikes I'd ever seen. Like a kid in a candy store, I spent over an hour wandering the hotel, marveling at these impressive machines. With a permanent grin on my face, I went back to my room to do some final preparation for my talk. My glee quickly turned to horror as I started reviewing some of their company websites. Green text on a brown background, images of every size splattered throughout, and one even had a distracting, spinning ferris wheel on the home page!

How could businesses with such beautiful products have such terrible websites?

I see this all too often in almost every industry. There is a disconnect between the offline and online brands.

What about your products or services? I'm going to give you the benefit of the doubt and trust that they're top quality like the gorgeous bikes I just mentioned. But what about your website? Would I be equally impressed, or is there a quality disconnect?

Take Action!

Go to www.SocialMediaOverload.com and click on Website Review to submit your site for a free, quick review from one of our professionals.

Four Website Pitfalls

These are the most common mistakes that I see in websites:

- Color pollution
- All images, no content
- Critical information is below the fold
- No opt-in box

Color Pollution

Color pollution can best be described by the "does it make my head spin" test we perform on every site we review. If you're looking for specifics, do not use more than three main colors on your site, more than two different fonts, and two or more animations (video, slideshow, and so on).

As with most things, the KISS (Keep It Simple, Sally) method still reigns supreme. A white background with black text, a few attractive images, and compelling content is all you need. Anything more than that and you might risk distracting or frustrating your visitors. Distracted or frustrated customers leave.

All Images, No Content

Another issue we see with many websites is having too many images and very little content. Content is critical for two reasons. First, it helps to tell a visitor who you are and what you do. If they can't figure that out quickly, they'll leave you and visit your competition. Content is also important to the search engines. That's what they use for figuring out who you are and what you do so that they'll know where to rank you on their search results. Websites that are purely image-based are frustrating to both visitors and search engines. For your homepage, have one or two paragraphs of content that clearly describe who you are and the products or services you provide. If you want bonus points, include internal links so people can easily visit pages within your site to see more information about the topic.

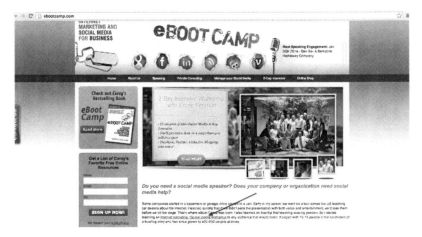

Critical Information Below the Fold

Did you know that 29.7 percent of people do not scroll down on websites? Did you also know that 87.4 percent of statistics are made-up on the spot? Wait for it...okay, if you didn't laugh, read it again. Seriously, I have no idea how many people scroll down on websites, but I know for certain that they have a better chance of seeing your critical information if you do not make them scroll. So what is your critical information? Your phone number? Physical address? A purchase option? Whatever it is, put it in a spot that can be seen on a gigantic flat-screen TV or on a tiny little smartphone. Do the three-second test to see if people can find this critical information in less than three seconds. If not, consider moving it to a more prominent position on your site.

Now, some people will say, "Corey, I have a Contact Us button on my site. Is that enough?" The problem with this button is that if I'm browsing your website with a smartphone, it's a bit of a pain to use my fat fingers to click on the contact link and find the phone number. If I'm on the go and I want to reach you, let me do a single-action click on the phone number to give you a call. Make it easy for me to spend money with you.

No Opt-In Box

This is definitely the most important piece of this chapter and possibly the entire book. I would like you to burn this acronym into your brain: **ABCE - Always Be Collecting Emails.** We have failed as marketers when we let someone visit our website and leave without giving us his or her information. At this point, we've already potentially lost that person as a customer. He will have to remember to come back to us when he is ready to purchase. I am not willing to take that chance. Instead, I want to collect his contact information and stay on his radar until he has made a decision.

Our goal, then, is to collect a visitor's information when he or she visits our website. The challenge, of course, is that people do not like to give away their information. We must give them a compelling reason to do so. That might be by offering a report to help them through the buying process or an exclusive discount that is delivered only via email. Something that is appealing enough so that they'll give away their precious contact info.

Best Practice: Less is More

The more information you ask for, the less likely someone will give it to you. So, only ask for the critical information you need to stay in touch with them. Name, email and phone number are generally the most important for staying in touch. It's okay to ask for more, but just remember that every additional field can deter your customer from signing up.

Case Study

We had a gentleman in one of our two-day eBoot Camps who let us put his website up on the big screen for a live review. We noticed that he did not have an opt-in box on his homepage to collect visitors' information. He emailed his web programmer and had it changed during the two days he was with us. He attended as a graduate a year later and told the class that this little change resulted in a 30 percent increase in web leads, which resulted in more than $100,000 in additional revenue.

FAQ: How important is it to have
a mobile-responsive website?

Quick answer: Very. If you have a website that shrinks down to fit your device, that's the bare minimum and a so-so option. I would much rather you have a site smart enough to recognize the device that the person is on and then change its functionality accordingly. To see an example, go to www.grennanconstruction.com on a computer and then go to the same site on your phone. I've included the mobile version below. You will see that the site changes to work better with your thumbs on your mobile device. If you haven't gotten there yet, that's where you should look to go, and sooner rather than later.

7

GOOGLE+ LOCAL BUSINESS

THIS CHAPTER COULD FALL under both "lead generation" as well as "building credibility" because it serves both purposes. If you do a Google search for a particular service in a particuler city and state (example: dentist Dallas, Texas), you will most likely see one or more directories on the first page.

If the search is on Google, visitors will most likely see Google's own directory—Google+ Local Business. Google+ Local gets a lot of prime real estate and if you own or work for a brick-and-mortar company, you will want to take this chapter very seriously. People often visit these pages first, and this is your opportunity to make a great first impression.

Example of a Google search displaying Google+ Local business listings:

If you have a local business with a physical address, Google gives you a free page. People often look at these Google-generated sites before getting directed to your website. Like your website, you get to choose what's on there. If you have not updated this page, it most likely looks something like this:

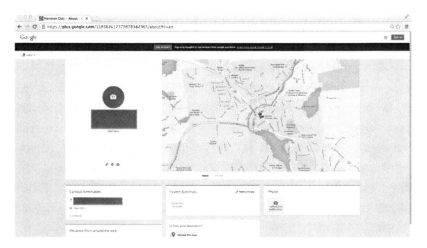

But it can look like this!

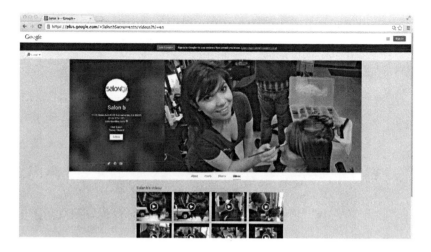

You have the opportunity to add critical information about your business on this page so people don't have to spend time searching for it. You can also add photos and videos to help your page stand out from your competition. People trust these pages, and here's why: they are looking at it on Google, not on your website, which adds a level of credibility. If it's on Google, it must be true, right?

The first step is to claim ownership of your Google+ Local page. Find your Google+ Local page by going to Google and typing in the name of your business with the city and state where it's located. Once directed to the correct page, you should see a big button that asks if you're the owner of this business. Follow the steps to claim the page as the owner or as the representative of the owner. An automated service from Google will call you and give you a pin number or mail a postcard that you can return to prove that you are the owner. Once you've claimed it, you can update it. You can start to add information, pictures, and video.

Imagine if you were searching for a chiropractor and you found this page which includes a virtual office tour and a video of the chiropractor demonstrating how she does adjustments. This might be just what you need to make your decision.

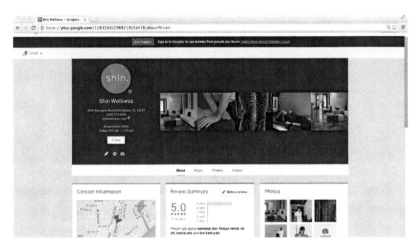

Google also allows you to add categories to your Google+ page. During a private consultation for a car dealership, I noticed that "used cars" was not one of the company's listed categories. This was a critical area of this business, yet it was missing from an important piece of online real estate.

Take Action!
Claim ownership of the page and make it beautiful

Reviews
Once you have claimed ownership and updated your page, you are halfway done. You should concentrate the remainder of your efforts on the review section of your Google+

Local business page. People can review your business on your page, and that review will be public whether you like it or not. Without sounding too dramatic, these reviews can literally make or break your business. As you read this, businesses are losing customers because of a negative review. And many times, the business has no idea that the review is even out there. So, the first step is to check your Google+ Local business page. How many reviews do you have? Any negative? If you don't have any reviews, you should consider yourself lucky. If just one person had left a negative review about your business, it would have stood alone and potentially swayed people from doing business with you.

Just do a quick local search for a dentist, salon, or restaurant, and you will quickly see that people can be quite nasty and seem to have way too much spare time—especially when perched behind a computer screen. I often compare the computer to beer. People say things when they're intoxicated that they would never say when sober. Same thing here. They spit fire behind the screen and then they're saints when you meet them face to face. But it's not going to go away. We need to be proactive instead of reactive. You can ignore negative reviews and risk losing business or you can do something about them.

Example of a page overwhelmed by bad reviews:

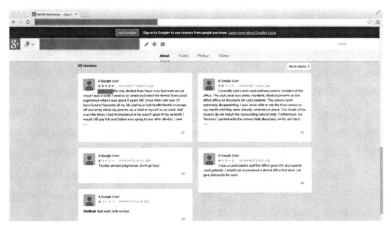

Take Action!

Ask your champion customers to write a review for you on your Google+ page.

Let me be very clear. I'm not suggesting that you ask your sister-in-law to write a glowing review for you. I'm suggesting that if a person is gushing about how great a job you did, you should ask that person to share those kind words on your Google+ page. Unfortunately, people are often much more motivated to write reviews when they are unhappy rather than when they are happy. So you might need to ask or remind the happy ones—and I see nothing wrong with that.

Best Practice: Get More Reviews

Here is a list of great ways to request reviews:

- A delivery slip or invoice
- In your store near the register

- Email blast to customers
- Via your social media sites

The key to all of these suggestions is timeliness. My wife recently got a massage and had an email waiting for her as soon as she got home. It was perfect timing because she was still happy and relaxed. Had they sent it twenty-four hours later, she would not have been nearly as motivated.

FAQ: How do I instruct my customers to write a review on Google?

Offering specific instructions would be futile because Google frequently changes the layout of these pages. Instead, I recommend that you go out and review another business sometime this week. Leave a great review for a restaurant you enjoyed, hair salon you love, or car dealership that's always treated you well. You'll feel good about doing it, and you'll know exactly how to proceed so that you can educate your customers. Win/win. Do this often so that you are up-to-date on Google+'s newest formats.

FAQ: Should I respond to negative reviews?

Yes. But first, sleep on it. Take all the emotion out of it and respond strategically and diplomatically. Try to make the situation better and turn the critic into a champion. People respect a business that makes an effort in customer satisfaction.

I once had a nasty review written about my first book. I cried myself to sleep over it! The next day, I woke up and contacted the person to discuss it. We had a lengthy phone conversation. He appreciated my willingness to listen to him, and he got a better perspective on my target audience and why I kept the book so simple. He even invited me to speak at one of his future events!

Now, if the review is just plain wrong, you certainly have the right to defend yourself. I would still be very careful though, not to come across as either defensive or offensive. Some reviewers are looking for a fight and would love to engage you in a war of words. That is exactly what you don't want to have happen.

You might be thinking that this does not apply to you because reviews aren't common in your industry. My rule of thumb is that if you have a Google+ Local business page, why wouldn't you ask your best customers to write a review for you? You never know when someone—right or wrong—may decide to publicly criticize your business. If that review is up against 15 positive ones, people might not pay attention to it. But if it is the lone review, I promise that they will.

Local Directories

Of course, Google is not the only game in town. There are other directories that offer you the opportunity to have a presence on their site. Some that come to mind are Yelp.com, UrbanSpoon.com, Kudzu.com, AngiesList.com, and those just scratch the surface. My suggestion is to do some Google searches around your product or service and your geographical location. If a directory ranks on the first or second page, I'd recommend spending some time on it and doing what you can to make it look good. Some directories have different rules than others. For example, Yelp.com does not want you soliciting reviews from your customers. In fact, they will try to filter out the review if they believe it was solicited by the business owner. So you will have to figure out what the rules are for each directory you select. But remember: if it ranks, pay attention to it. If it doesn't, I would put it at the bottom of your priority list.

8

NUMBERS MATTER

IF YOU LOOK BACK at our social media sales funnel, we are still in the "building credibility" phase. When it comes to social media profiles, nothing can diminish your credibility faster than an untouched profile. If your LinkedIn profile has 21 connections, no headshot, and has not had an update since 2012, what does it say about you? At a recent event, I asked the audience what goes through their heads when they visit a Facebook business page with very few fans and that hasn't been updated in months. One woman responded, "I just leave—I figure they went out of business."

I would rather you delete the profile than just let it sit there and collect dust.

This goes back to one of the fundamentals I previously mentioned. You need to decide on the social media sites you are going to focus on and get rid of the rest. As years go on, you can always add new profiles as you choose, but just make sure there is a plan to manage them and stick to that plan.

Take Action!

Take inventory of all the profiles you have online. Are there any that currently are not being managed?

If yes, decide right now whether to create a plan for managing them or to delete the profile.

FAQ: What's the right number of fans, followers, or connections in order to have credibility with a visitor?

I find that it really depends on your industry. If you are a commercial construction company, a few hundred Facebook fans is probably fine. If you are a restaurant in downtown Chicago, you probably want thousands. When it comes to a personal LinkedIn profile, I often challenge people to get to at least 500 connections. I believe everyone can reach this number without sacrificing the quality of the people they are connecting with. Most of you know 500 people in this giant networking party we call planet earth. We just need to do a bit of work on LinkedIn to connect with them.

You do not need to connect with complete strangers to get to the 500 mark.

If 500+ seems too daunting, go for 250 connections. I think that is a perfectly suitable number for most people to get, and it will keep you looking favorable in the eyes of those who visit your profile.

Best Practice: Become More Popular

Here are a few ways to generate more likes, friends, followers, and connections:

Blast an email to your list requesting that they join you on your social media profiles. Don't just ask them to do it, give them a compelling reason, such as something free, a discount, or a contest with a cool prize.

Add social media icons to your website. Again, simply adding icons will probably offer low-to-moderate results. Think of a creative way to get people excited about staying connected to you on social media. You can do this by offering something or sharing the value that they will receive once they join.

Get them offline. Do you have a store, classroom, or office where customers and prospects visit? Pretend that your doors are a turnstile and get every one of them to join your social media sites. Offer incentives or value to get them to take the time to do it. Also, make it really simple by having a sign with the exact steps on how to join.

Cross-promote. Ask your LinkedIn connections to become Facebook fans and ask your Twitter followers to connect on Instagram. When you really embrace social media, you have different relationships with your network based on where they are connected with you. On Twitter, your involvement might just be the occasional announcement or mention, but on Instagram or Pinterest, you might share your latest product line or show off your favorite customers.

Try not to get too caught up in inflating your numbers though, as this can become overwhelming and distracting. I don't believe in just building your numbers just for the sake of looking big or busy. I want you to concentrate on building a "connected" network of people on each profile you decide to focus on. A by-product of that will be people visiting these profiles and hopefully noticing how active and popular you are. We all know that first impressions are important, and offering a vibrant profile with a large network is a step in the positive direction.

9

LET YOUR LINKEDIN PROFILE SELL FOR YOU

I REMEMBER BEING AT a car dealership with my dad and watching him kick the tire of one of the cars he was thinking about purchasing. When I asked him what he was doing, he laughed, leaned over, and said to me, "I have no idea, but I saw your granddad do it once!" I now know that my dad (and his dad) were trying to assess the quality of that car by kicking the tire. On the web, prospects kick our tires by checking out our LinkedIn profile. They can easily see details about us and our company. This chapter will offer some ways for you to give off a great first impression when people visit your LinkedIn profile.

Add a Professional, Current Photo

This seems simple, but it is often overlooked. I still see hundreds of profiles with blurry photos, or worse, with no photo at all. It sends off warning signals to people thinking of buying from you. Why risk that? Get a photo up there that you are proud of and that's a good representation of your company.

Carefully Choose Your Title

Right below your name is your first opportunity to sell someone on your value. Do not just put a boring, standard title there like "real estate agent" or "mortgage broker," but instead add some sizzle! For example, look at my friend Terry Brock's profile—www.linkedin.com/in/marketerterrybrock. As soon as his new book came out, he changed his title to highlight the big announcement. Just by looking at his name, he has already begun to build credibility with visitors. What can you add to your name or title to help your profile stand out?

Best Practice: Don't Forget Your Distinctions

On Terry's profile, you will also notice he takes advantage of the space next to his name to share his speaking credentials. If you have earned the right to add a distinction or certification that would be impressive to others and give you credibility, make sure you add it to your profile.

Add a Professional Summary with the Readers' Interests in Mind

Unless you're looking for a job, your profile is not a resume. So don't treat it like one by talking about yourself and your qualifications. Instead, focus on how you help others or the benefits your company provides. If I am viewing a real estate agent's profile, for example, I don't want to read about their past experiences or general biographic information. I want to see the statistics on some of the houses they have sold and how they're going to get my house sold quickly! The sooner you can direct your summary toward the person reading it, the more engaged and excited they will be to meet you!

Best Practice: Bring Your Profile to Life

LinkedIn also allows you to upload multimedia options to your profile. You can upload a video from YouTube, a PowerPoint presentation from SlideShare, or just some photos from your website. It's a great way to help your profile stand out from your competition! To see an example, check out www.LinkedIn.com/in/CoreyPerlman and connect with me while you're there!

Best Practice: Get Quality Recommendations from Past Clients

When it comes to recommendations, it's quality over quantity. If you ask the right people to recommend you on LinkedIn, they will spend time crafting an endorsement worthy of the exceptional product or service you offer. Recommendations matter.

No, scratch that...

Quality recommendations matter. These should come from people who have used your products or services and have had an exceptional experience. They will share insights that will generate buying signals for your prospects when they read the recommendation.

FAQ: What's up with these endorsements? Should I care about them? Why are people endorsing me for things I don't even do?

Endorsements are supposed to be a verification tool for your different skill sets. The more people who endorse you for a skill, the more likely you are to have that skill.

I'm not sure why people are endorsing you for skills you don't really have. You should ask them!

I'm not even sure LinkedIn knows exactly what it is going to do with endorsements, but I do think it is worth paying attention to them. My guess is that LinkedIn will end up using endorsements as a search ranking tool for the site. So if you were searching for "social media expert" on LinkedIn, and I had more endorsements than Sally Smith (made-up name), I would rank higher on the page than she would. That could prove to be important down the road.

Best Practice: Update Your Profile Daily

This takes little to no time at all, but could result in significantly more business. Go check out your LinkedIn profile. You will notice some updates from a few of your contacts. These are people who have posted updates to their profiles and did it right around the time of your visit. If you are in "buy mode" for their products or services at the time of their posting, this could be the friendly reminder that earns them your business.

The same goes for your prospects. They could be in need of what you can offer, but you may have fallen off their radar for one reason or another. During a visit to LinkedIn, they see a status update from you referencing a great article on leadership from the *Harvard Business Review*. Whether they read the article or not is irrelevant. The point is that you jumped back on their radar at precisely the right time and a sale could be made.

This strategy has become even more important with LinkedIn's mobile app. If you don't already have it, I encourage you to download it. When you first open it up, updates from your network will be the first thing that you'll see. This is prime real estate, and you can take advantage of this opportunity by simply adding high-value content to your LinkedIn profile.

Here is a view of the app from my phone and the status updates that appeared:

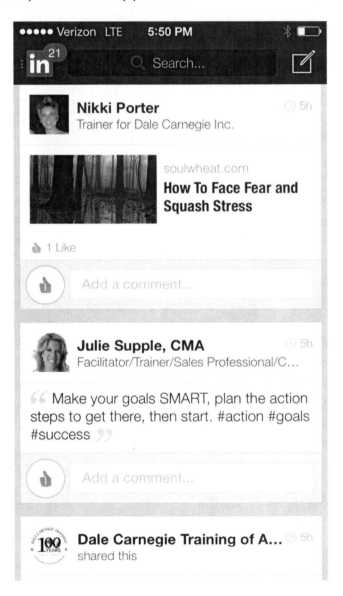

Best Practice: Get to that 500+ Connections Mark
It is an easy club to get into and you don't even have to pay to be a member! All you need to do is spend some time actively seeking out people you know on LinkedIn and invite them to connect. In no time at all, you will start getting closer to that magic number and without having to connect with total strangers. You will be amazed how many people you know with whom you simply forgot to connect. Once you hit 500, LinkedIn stops displaying your actual number of connections. So you could have 501 or 5,001, and it will still just say 500+ on your profile. A by-product of doing this exercise is that you will have a comprehensive network on LinkedIn. This will pay dividends for you when we explore other LinkedIn strategies.

SECTION FOUR

STAY "TOP OF MIND"

UNFORTUNATELY, OUR PROSPECTS DON'T wake up every day thinking about us.

For almost two years, a guy named Milo attempted to sell me life insurance. He would call me, send me emails, and we even met for lunch a few times. I just wasn't remotely interested. After months of follow-up, he finally stopped trying. A few years later, I had a daughter. I woke up one morning, in a cold sweat, thinking how much of a negligent father I was because I did not have life insurance in case something happened to me. Good news for Milo, right? Wrong. I had totally forgotten about him.

I planned on going to Google to search for a company that sold life insurance. As usual, my ADD kicked in and I found myself popping over to LinkedIn for a moment before I started my research. I was skimming the news feed and saw an excellent Dale Carnegie quote about worry and stress. Perfect for a guy who is already stressing about his four-year-old daughter's first date! Guess who posted the great, inspirational quote? You got it, Milo did. I clicked on his profile and sent him a direct email that stated, "I'm finally ready to buy life insurance." He was able to be Top of Mind with me when I was finally ready to buy. Not by annoying me with constant follow up, but simply by being connected to me on LinkedIn.

Of all the different benefits of social media and digital marketing, staying Top of Mind might be my favorite and most underutilized of the bunch. We often meet people months before we end up doing business together. The challenge is staying on their radar (without annoying them) until they are ready to buy from us. This could be a month from now or a year from now. Today, people go to the web for information. If we can be one of the sources of that information, then we have a much better chance of staying Top of Mind with them and eventually earning their business.

Being Top of Mind is equally important with existing customers. If we are only showing up on their radar when it's invoice time, then that is a recipe for a short relationship. Instead, think about how we can have multiple points of contact with them throughout the month while offering value along the way that can help their business. It has been our experience that the more positive communication we have with our clients, the better the relationship.

The next few chapters will cover some of the best areas on the web that you can use to stay Top of Mind with your customers and prospects. These include:

- Email Marketing
- Blogging
- Social Media Updates

The two most important words in this section will be consistency and value. If you accomplish both, you should have great success.

10

EMAIL MARKETING

WHEN I COVER THIS section in my presentations, I always ask the audience how many of them have checked their email today. Every hand goes up. So contrary to the opinion of many social media experts out there, email is far from dead.

The problem is not whether people are reading emails or not; the challenge is getting them to read yours.

It is extremely difficult to get your email read because of the tough spam filters and the amount of junk mail people receive in their email inboxes. We must be more creative and strategic in our approach than ever before.

FAQ: How often should I email my contacts?

My answer is always the same: **I care less about frequency, and more about value.**

I get an email from Mashable.com every day. Christmas, Hanukkah, my birthday, it doesn't matter—I get an email from them. But it's good stuff, so I will never unsubscribe. At the same time, if I get an email once a quarter and it's not valuable to me, I will unsubscribe right away. So we must focus on the value that we're putting in our emails.

Value > Frequency

How can we make the subject line so enticing that people have to open our email?

What can we put in the header that will make them want to read the entire email?

If they would like to get more involved with us, what call to action can we offer that will help them take the next step?

Did you catch that last one? It is extremely important and something we will cover in great detail in Chapter Thirteen, "How to Get Them to Your Sweet Spot." Every email should have a strong call to action so readers will know what to do if they are ready to buy or want to get more information. It's the most common section that's missing in most email marketing pieces, and it can mean the difference between a successful email campaign and a failed one.

Best Practice: ABCE (Always Be Collecting Emails)

Of course, none of this matters if you are not actively collecting emails. If you have an active email campaign, you'll naturally lose some people along the way. You need to be consistently adding to your list so that you don't run out of subscribers. If you go back to Section One about generating leads, you will want to make sure that, at a minimum, you are collecting people's email addresses so you can stay Top of Mind with them.

From this point forward, you will never do a lead-generation campaign without collecting your readers' email addresses as part of the process.

For most of us, collecting email addresses (and other contact info) is the lifeblood of our business. It is the starting point in most sales situations, and shame on us if we encounter a prospect and neglect to collect an email address.

But you can't stop there. Simply collecting business cards is not going to get the job done. If you have a value-rich email marketing campaign, you can stay Top of Mind and build credibility until prospects become your customers down the road.

Best Practice: Watch Your Open Rate

There's a reason we use services like ConstantContact.com, MailChimp.com, or ExactTarget.com–they give us the ability to track how many people open and interact with our emails. Watch these numbers carefully and adjust accordingly. Based on these results, you can change subject lines, rearrange articles, and offer a more appealing call to action.

FAQ: Should I buy email lists?

I get this one a lot. I'm not a big fan of buying lists—I think it crosses over the spam line because people did not originally give you permission to email them. I know other marketers might disagree with this, but it's my take. My clients have asked me to buy lists for them numerous times and I have always declined. I would rather see you focus on building your list organically with the strategies we have already discussed.

11

BLOGGING TOWARD THOUGHT LEADERSHIP

WHEN I EXPLAIN BLOGS, I typically describe them as an online magazine for your business. Imagine someone walking into your office and sitting in the lobby. She looks down at the table and sees a magazine that has your business name on it. Inside, there are articles all relating to your industry, and this person (hopefully a prospect) finds this information very interesting. If you took that content and slapped it online, that would be your business blog.

I remember when a client told me that he once visited an executive with whom he was hoping to do business. As he walked into her office, he looked at her desk and noticed that one of his articles from his blog was on it. She saw his eyes focusing on the article, and told him that she had printed a copy for all of her employees. The sale was made even before he walked through the door.

Not only can a blog keep you Top of Mind with prospects and customers, it can also help establish you as a thought leader in your industry. Unlike a social media profile, a blog is typically made up of articles and, therefore, gives you a lot more room to share your knowledge and viewpoint.

The negative side of maintaining a blog is that it's time intensive. It typically takes our team an hour or two to create a good blog article and we recommend at least one article per week in order for your blog to develop any sort of readership or return. But, I have good news. If you can get someone (it does not necessarily need to be you) to write one quality article per week, you can use that content throughout your digital marketing channels.

You can take that single blog article and use it as the main content of your email marketing piece. You can then "chunk up" (my made-up phrase!) the article and use it on your social media channels. And if you really want to get fancy, you could record it as a YouTube video or create an infographic and put it on Instagram. The point is that you can get a lot of mileage out of one blog article.

TURN YOUR
BLOG ARTICLE
into a Week's Worth of Content

Best Practice: "If You Write It, They Will Come" Is a Myth
Just because you've written a great blog article, that doesn't mean it is going to create a big splash on the digital scene. You must shove it—and I really do mean shove it—down the throats of readers before it starts to gain traction. Here are a few tips to getting more blog readers:

- Blast an email to every human being you know and share your article with them. If you are not willing to do that, then maybe the article is not worth reading?
- Add the link to all of your social media profiles AND get your employees to do the same thing.

- Use a compelling title and subtitle. People are busy so you need to capture their attention right away. Going negative always seems to work well. For example, learning five ways to avoid a flooded basement is something I might read. How to properly seal a basement is not as appealing.
- Get social. Make sure you have all the cool "share" tabs on your blog articles. If someone wants to share it on Facebook, LinkedIn, or Twitter, give them an easy way to do it.
- Use bullets. At eBoot Camp, we've literally written thousands of blog articles for clients, and have found that using bullets—"Five tips," "Seven strategies," or "Nine ways"— get many more reads than just paragraphs of content.

Don't Just Phone It In

Don't write a blog article just to have something up there. Make a difference. Help people. The better your article, the more it will be read and shared. I always recommend that companies have social media meetings (more on this later) where you brainstorm about good blog topics. This will produce lots of good things to write about.

You can also create a content calendar. This way, you are not always looking for a new topic to write about. You can use the meeting I just mentioned to create your four topics for the month, and then all you need to do is to write them.

FAQ: What if I just do not have time to write?

Here are a few ways you can leverage other people when you can't find time to write.

Use guest writers. There are a lot of talented people who love to write and who would like to get increased exposure through your blog. If you mention this to enough people in your network, you will start to create some opportunities that will be a win/win for both of you. You will get some great content that is valuable to your audience, and the writer will get some nice exposure.

Use www.Zerys.com. This is an article marketplace. You can ask for an article you would like written and the amount you are willing to pay. Writers will submit articles to you and you only pay for the one you end up using. Pretty cool!

Use your employees! I have some of the most talented employees in the world. In fact, one often writes my blog. Fire yourself from writing and let others express their expertise on your topic. You will be surprised at just how good they are—sometimes even better than you.

12

SOCIAL MEDIA UPDATES

IF YOU GO BACK to my story at the beginning of this section, you'll remember that the life insurance salesman got my business because of a simple LinkedIn post. This is low-hanging fruit that many of you are missing. You may have done a great job connecting to all of your customers and prospects on sites like LinkedIn, but you're not updating it consistently with high-value content. Shame on you! Right now, go log in to your LinkedIn account. Right next to your profile picture is a status box where you can share an update. When you hit "share," the update appears at the top of all of your connections' news feeds. If they happen to be on LinkedIn as well, they have an excellent chance of seeing your post. The goal is two-fold: jump on their radar and, if possible, build credibility through the value of your post.

During my presentations, I often show my LinkedIn homepage and the status updates from my connections that appear at the very top of the page. I make the joke that I can drive down any highway and Verizon is paying a gazillion dollars to try to get my attention while Deb Stevenson just got it by simply posting to LinkedIn! So if you're not already doing it, get in the habit of posting high-value content to your social media profiles.

Worth repeating: if you're not already doing it, get in the habit of posting high-value content to your social media profiles.

It will help you stay Top of Mind with the people to whom you are connected.

FAQ: What should I post?

Whatever your customers or prospects deem valuable.

Here are some suggestions to get you started:

Share a great article that you read. Simply copy and paste the link, share why you found it valuable, and post the link.

Answer questions. You met with a client, and they brought up a question or challenge that others might also be wondering about. Share the issue and how you addressed it.

Tell stories. People love good stories. Share an experience you had with a customer and how you helped her.

Use pictures. Yes, they are indeed worth a thousand words. Used in the right way, pictures can really garner the attention of your connections and get some great engagement.

Don't be afraid of soft promotion. I will be addressing your Sweet Spot soon, but for now, just know that it's okay to share some things you or your business are doing. Just don't overdo it. If you have a great sale going on, mention it! If you have an event coming up, feel free to use social media to invite them.

FAQ: How often should I post?

At a minimum, I recommend daily posts to social media sites like Facebook, LinkedIn, and Twitter. Unless someone is on the site when you post, chances are fairly low that they will even see your update. Therefore, you must post frequently in order to see any kind of results. The only time I've heard of people getting frustrated by over-posting is when someone "cluster posts." This is where you share multiple updates at the same time and clutter people's news feeds with your content. It is annoying and you could lose connections by committing this social media sin. If you are just beginning, try to update your social media sites a few times a week. Once that becomes routine, feel free to increase to daily updates.

Beware! If you are finding that your social media sites are not getting updated, I would advise you to find someone who can keep them active or delete the unused account.

Best Practice: Brag about Your Customers

This is a great way to show appreciation to some of your customers and softly promote your products and services at the same time. An example might be highlighting a customer that saved money by using your services or publicly thanking a customer for their testimonial.

FAQ: How can I get more comments on my posts?

Getting people to comment on your posts is never easy. I was once doing a private consultation with a hair salon, and the owner kept mentioning things she had seen on my Facebook business page. I was really surprised she had seen so many of our posts because she'd never commented on a single one. When I asked her about it, she said, "Corey, I will never comment on your business page. If I do, all of your fans can see me and click on my profile. No, thank you!"

Wow, I was stunned that she felt that way. How many other people feel the same?

Nonetheless, comments are still important to get and help spread your content organically. I liken getting your first comment to getting the first dancers on the dance floor at a wedding. It's never easy, but once a few daring couples get out there, the rest follow. I suggest asking a few people to be your "first dancers." Get friends, co-workers, or others to comment on some of your posts to get the dialogue going. Once others see people chiming in, they might be more apt to join the conversation.

SECTION FIVE

FROM SOCIAL MEDIA TO YOUR SWEET SPOT

DRIVE PEOPLE TOWARD YOUR SWEET SPOT

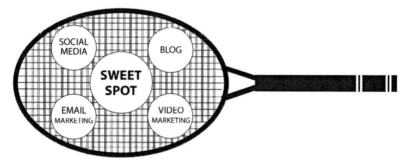

I WAS IN A ROOM with about twelve people from a roofing company. We had spent the past three hours discussing exactly how they would use the web to grow their business. One gentleman raised his hand and said, "Corey, this is all great, but at the end of the day, we want to sell more roofs. Do we sell them on Facebook, Twitter, or our website?"

I asked the group if there was an easy access to the roof of the building. They looked at me inquisitively and then pointed to a door at the end of the hallway. I asked them to lead me out on the roof. They scampered out on the roof with grace and ease. For me, it was a little less graceful. In suit and tie, I carefully took one step at a time and remained on all fours until I met the guys in the center of the extremely pitched roof.

"What are we doing out here?" one of the roofers asked.

"Well, you asked me where you sell more roofs," I said. Pointing at the roof, I finished, "This is where you sell more roofs—the same place you always have. You're going to use the web to generate more leads, build credibility, and stay Top of Mind, but you're still going to offer free estimates, demonstrate the benefits of getting a new roof, and close the deal right here."

If you are a doctor, your sweet spot is in your office. If you sell IT services, your sweet spot is in the prospect's office. That won't change just because you are using social media.

Don't sell on social media; drive people to your sweet spot.

Your organization needs to determine where your sweet spot is. Discuss it with your entire team to gather input and gain consensus. If one department is sending email blasts and another is doing a Twitter campaign, both need to be clear on where to direct people. This will help you see actual results from your digital marketing strategies.

13

WHERE'S YOUR SWEET SPOT?

SOME OF OUR FAVORITE and long-standing clients are Dale Carnegie franchises from around the world. Dale Carnegie offers professional development solutions for individuals and businesses, and has been successfully doing so for more than 100 years. We learned early on that social media was not the place to sell their public programs. We needed to get people to Dale Carnegie's sweet spot...the classroom. Once there, people experienced the true value of a Dale Carnegie program and were more likely to invest in and continue with the program. Dale Carnegie franchises were smart enough to allow people to attend a session for free, and we simply invited people to attend via social media.

People love free.

You can also have multiple sweet spots. Another client, a bathroom remodeling company, often has in-store displays at companies like Lowes and Home Depot, both of which are their sweet spots!

The key is knowing where you have the best chance to show your value to your prospects.

E-commerce sites, like Amazon.com, know that their sweet spots are specific pages on their website. It is not their homepage, but the individual product pages that make up their sweet spots. Therefore, they use social media and digital marketing strategies to drive more people to those pages.

Take Action!

Spend some time figuring out the exact location of your sweet spot.

Is there one location or multiple locations?

Discuss this with your team. Make sure everyone is in agreement on where your sweet spot is and if there are multiple sweet spots for your different products or services.

Best Practice: Sell or Suffer the Consequences

Still a little confused on exactly where your sweet spot is? Pretend I have your precious iPhone12 (are we on version 12 yet?) held hostage and plan to toss it in my blender and hit the smoothie button if you don't sell something today. What will you do? Will you get on the phone and make calls? Will you set appointments? Will you drive to multiple businesses? This exercise will help you determine your sweet spot.

14

EVERYTHING, AND I MEAN EVERYTHING, SHOULD LEAD TO YOUR SWEET SPOT

WHAT DO YOU CURRENTLY have online that is not directing people to your sweet spot?

That needs to be fixed immediately! Do an audit of all your marketing—both online and offline—and make sure each is doing the job of driving people to your sweet spot.

FAQ: What's the difference between your sweet spot and a call to action?

Your sweet spot is the destination, and a call to action is how people get there. You need to have a strong call to action in order to have success in getting prospects to your sweet spot. Don't be afraid to try different things. One of my sweet spots is on stage at a workshop or keynote presentation. In our weekly eNewsletter, we offer incentives for people to come see me at one of these events. We track these offers to see how they do and make changes accordingly.

FAQ: Is it okay to simply direct them to my sweet spot or do I need to offer some kind of incentive?

In the previous chapter, I shared an example of in-store displays for a bathroom remodeling company. If we simply would have told the prospects that the company was at Lowes or Home Depot, we would have received very little response. Instead of just telling people to go visit the remodeler at their neighborhood store, we told them to go spin the Wheel of Fun for prizes like store gift cards, kids toys, and big discounts toward a bathroom makeover.

You need to have a strategy for driving people to your sweet spot. How can you make it fun and less sales-y? You will want to convey this strategy across all departments so everyone is on the same page.

FAQ: How do we track the effectiveness of each strategy?

I once held a public social media event and sold tickets for $197. I promoted the event on Facebook and told my fans that if they came to the event and screamed FACEBOOK as loud as they could when they registered, they could get in for half price. The best part was that I didn't tell my registration team about the deal. People would walk up and scream in the faces of my employees and scare the heck out of them. It was great fun, and I got to see my marketing at work.

Give specific instructions on each digital tool you're using, and you will quickly see where your leads are coming from.

Case Study

They say life starts right outside your comfort zone. Two years ago, I walked into a Brazilian jiu jitsu school to learn something brand new. I have been hooked ever since. The master instructor (we call him Sifu) has become a fitness mentor for me and a friend. We talk about life and business quite a bit at the local coffee shop. During one of our conversations, I asked Sifu where he thought his sweet spot was. He immediately replied, "The mat, of course," referring to the mat his students work out on. "Once they get on the mat, the experience sells itself," he said. I suggested he should be more specific. I told him that it took me years to work up the courage to step on the mat. My hesitation was less about the price and more about the unknown.

So what could Sifu do to bring new people in without the fear of injury, of having to commit long term, or whatever their fear is? We agreed that a more specific sweet spot might be his self-defense seminars or free workshops. These options are low-priced, one-time events with no long-term commitment. It eliminates the major concerns people have and gets more prospects in the door. And again, after you come in once, you will likely want to return.

It is important to be really specific about where your sweet spot is since that will dictate how you implement your digital marketing. For the jiu jitsu school, instead of marketing their monthly plans, the school decided to focus on endorsing their workshops and seminars, which were easier for people to say yes to.

It was a slight change that made a big difference.

Sifu may be a black belt in jiu jitsu, but he still has some work to do to get his black belt in social media. I will most certainly get a good collar choke after he reads this.

Case Study

One of our clients helps insurance agents become more successful in their business. This client is extremely knowledgeable in her field and her passion shines through whenever she speaks. We quickly realized we needed to get her in front of her prospects in order for them to truly see the value of working with her. The challenge was that her prospects were all over the world. We decided a webinar would be a perfect venue for her to get the information across and in a meaningful and engaging way. Once we defined her sweet spot, the rest was easy. Every email we created, social media site we managed, or article we wrote all led people to register for this webinar. In the end, she had a great crowd show up for her online event and many eventually became clients.

To Sum it Up

It's probably because we recently welcomed a new son into the world, but I seem to be awfully emotional these days. I was with a client last week, and we were shooting some video segments to add to his YouTube page. Toward the end of the first video, my client asked, "Corey, how are we going to direct viewers to my sweet spot?" I had to take a moment to collect myself and dry my tears. I was so proud!

Whether it's a video, email piece, direct mail, or something else, all of these roads should lead toward your sweet spot. As you should see by now, all of these moving parts work together. That is the key to not getting overwhelmed (or overloaded!) as you add new marketing channels to your digital strategy.

SECTION SIX

Build Stronger Relationships with Your Customers

It's easier to keep a customer than to gain a new one. For you Jerry Maguire fans out there, I can picture his legendary mentor, Dicky Fox, saying that line over and over again. And I couldn't agree more with this fundamental principle.

By following the prior strategies, you've hopefully generated new leads through building credibility and staying Top of Mind, and you've turned those leads into customers. But you are not finished yet! No one likes to be treated like they are just another sale, and if you stop the communication after the contract is signed, that is exactly how the customer will feel. It's time to start building long-lasting relationships with your new customers. Staying in touch with them and checking in on how they are doing is key to keeping them as customers for the long term. When I have status meetings with my account managers, I always remind them of the importance of consistent communication with our clients. If a client complains about too much communication from us, I will not criticize my team. Too much communication is a much better problem to have than my clients feeling as if they are being ignored.

The tools might be changing, but the fundamentals remain the same. I've made a lot of mistakes in my business, but the one thing I've consistently done right is not underestimating the importance of building strong relationships with my clients. Because our clients span the globe, I've predominantly used the web to build those relationships. Do I think the web eliminates the need for face-to-face interaction? Of course not. Instead, I believe it is simply an additional opportunity to connect and communicate. The following chapters will offer some unique and new opportunities to build stronger relationships with your customers.

15

KEEP YOUR FRIENDS CLOSE AND YOUR CLIENTS EVEN CLOSER

WE ARE GOING TO start this chapter with a quick exercise, so please grab something to write with.

Write down the names of one or two VIP customers. What constitutes a VIP?

Well, a VIP could be someone who has been a client for a long time or who has invested a significant amount of money in your company. As a reminder, you are writing down people, not companies—so if you work with the company, write down the decision-maker's name.

1.

2.

Write down each of their birth dates:

1.

2.

Write down what distinctions you know about these clients. What achievements or awards have they won? If you walked into their office, what would they be displaying proudly on the wall?

1.

2.

What are their hobbies? What are their favorite things to do when they are not at work? Who are their favorite sports teams?

1.

2.

What are they passionate about? When they wake up each morning, what is one of the first things they think about?

1.

2.

Are you in consistent communication with them? This means, in some form or fashion, they hear from you once or twice a week. If yes, give examples.

1.

2.

How did you do? Is this important information to know about your VIP clients? I would think so.

I would like to introduce you to one of my VIP clients, Mary Stevenson.

Mary's birthday is May 11, and for her birthday I sent her some of the greatest chocolate in the world, from Sarasota, Florida, my hometown. She told me it was a huge hit with her staff and one of the best gifts she had ever received.

She just celebrated her tenth year of being cigarette-free.

I sent her a congratulations card through the mail and told her about my mother and her untimely death due to lung cancer. I expressed how proud of her I was for being able to kick such an addictive habit.

Mary is a huge Alabama Crimson Tide fan, so when they won their second consecutive national championship, I sent her a little University of Alabama elephant for her granddaughter with a note asking if they could take a year off so the Florida State Seminoles could win one! (Note: It worked! Go Noles!)

Speaking of her granddaughter, Mary and I have an ongoing battle over who has the cutest three year old. I think it's Talia, my daughter, and she thinks it's Layla, her granddaughter. It's a tight race.

I interact with Mary at least once a week. Besides being a friend and a wonderful lady, Mary is also my largest client.

So how do I know all this information about Mary? We are friends.

Specifically, we are friends on Facebook.

Let me be absolutely clear on this so there is no chance of confusion: I have one personal account on Facebook through which I have chosen to connect with some of my largest clients. In other words, I'm mixing my business life with my personal life.

Let's do a preemptive strike here and list some of your immediate FAQs:

FAQ: Are you asking me to allow business contacts to connect with me personally on Facebook? Are you crazy?

I am not asking you to do that, but I am suggesting that some of you take this step. This is not right for everyone. If you're not a Facebook user or a Facebook fan, then I don't think you should use this strategy. If you are an attorney, then you DEFINITELY shouldn't use this strategy.

This strategy is not for everyone.

But if you have repeat customers or long-term clients, this might be a great way to deepen your relationship with them.

FAQ: But can't they see everything on my profile?

Yes, they can, so you will need to clean it up if you still have those pictures of you taking a shot of peppermint schnapps out of an ice luge…or maybe that was just me. And you do lose the right to simply post anything you feel like. There are plenty of times I would like to vent about a politician or share a slightly inappropriate joke that my brother sent me, but I decide against it. I won't risk damaging the relationships I have with my clients.

FAQ: What if I have two profiles: one for my friends and one for my clients?

You can do that, but that's double the work. I am trying to help you become more efficient, so I would suggest just having one profile. In the real world, your business life is very much a part of your personal life—it is unavoidable. When we talk about our day at the dinner table, we talk about work. When we go out with friends, work is almost always a part of the conversation. If they are blended offline, why not blend them online?

FAQ: What if my friends get annoyed if I talk about business on my personal profile?

Then get rid of them! They are probably the same people you have been trying to get rid of since high school.

FAQ: What if I have employees who want to do this? How do I control what our clients see on their profiles?

This is a touchy subject and may require some legal guidance. I'm obviously not an attorney, so I'm not going to offer advice here. What I will say is that some guidelines need to be in place if your salespeople will be allowed to connect personally with your clients. I would suggest running it by your legal department or an attorney and be clear on your rights as the employer and their rights as the employee.

For some of you, the above challenges might be too much to overcome, and feel free to bail. I mean that. This strategy is not for everyone, and it does come with some major compromises that you might not be willing to make.

For me, the advantages far outweigh the disadvantages.

I'm able to connect with my clients on a deeper level by being connected with them on Facebook. How did I know Mary's birthday? As with all of my other Facebook friends, it showed up at the top of the page.

Mary also shares things on Facebook that she probably would not share with me in a typical business meeting. I'm able to share in Mary's successes and support her during challenging times.

Can this type of interaction happen on your Facebook business page? Absolutely not. How about LinkedIn? It just doesn't work that way. It's a personal Facebook page strategy.

I really hate calling it a strategy because you can't (or shouldn't) use it as a strategy. It will backfire and blow up in your face. You should only connect with a client on Facebook if you truly consider the person a friend. And you should only engage with something they posted on Facebook because it truly moved you, not for strategic purposes. The bottom line: just treat them as you do your other friends, and you'll be fine.

We are in a vastly different world than we were just a few years ago and privacy has changed dramatically. You can fight these changes and do what you can to limit your public persona or you can embrace it and find ways to deepen your relationship with your customers. I said it once and I will say it again, Facebook does not eliminate the need for face-to-face communication; it is simply another way to stay connected.

Best Practice: If You Can't Say Something Nice...

Resist the urge to vent. Recently, Frontier Airlines lost my luggage, and I was in a nasty mood about it. In a moment of weakness, I vented a bit on my personal page. Luckily, I wised up and deleted the rant before I posted it. Instead, I sent the airline a note on their Facebook business page, and they actually responded and helped me resolve my issue. No one wants to hear us hem and haw about our problems—they get enough of that from their kids! Resist the urge to be a negative Norm or Nancy on Facebook, and together we can make the digital world a more positive place.

Best Practice: Stick to Kosher Conversation

When I go to my in-laws' place for Thanksgiving, there are always certain subjects that we avoid. Politics is at the top of that list. If it's not kosher at the in-laws' Thanksgiving dinner table, it's definitely not appropriate on Facebook. Look, you're either going to piss off 49 percent or 51 percent of your audience, so why do it? Resist jumping on your political soapbox and stick to topics a bit less controversial—like religion! Just kidding.

Case Study

A few weeks ago, I had a scheduled phone meeting with my client and friend, Terry C. Here's how Terry began the call:

"Corey, before we get started, I want to let you know how great it is to see those pictures of you and your daughter that you post on Facebook. You're a wonderful, involved father, and it makes me proud to do business with you."

When I told this story on stage, I had a hard time getting through it because I became emotional. This was partly because I am madly in love with my children, but also because the fact that I am a good dad matters to my client. It is a wonderful reminder to me that, at the end of the day, it all boils down to relationships. We are lucky to live in a time when we have access to tools and technology that allow us to build deeper relationships with people. I do not hide who I am on Facebook just because I'm connected with my clients. They will see that I'm a die-hard Florida State Seminoles fan, a certified Parrot head, and a devoted husband and father. And that is perfectly fine with me.

16

THE ONE REASON
TO USE GOOGLE+

GOOGLE+ IS GOOGLE'S SOCIAL networking platform. It was developed to compete with Facebook, and as of this writing, it has not been very successful in gaining market share. I continue to ask my audiences around the country if they are actively using Google+, and very few hands go up. So why am I suggesting you use it?

Two Words: Google Hangouts

Google Hangouts is like Skype, except more robust and with more options. You can host a video conference with up to ten people in a Google Hangout. We use Google Hangouts with our clients from all over the world. Not only can we quickly have multiple people on the call, but Google allows you to easily record the sessions and post them directly to YouTube (also owned by Google).

The only requirement is . . . you guessed it. You must have a Google+ profile.

I'm all about efficiency and prioritization, so I put Google+ behind Facebook, LinkedIn, and Twitter. However, if you're looking for a way to communicate more effectively with customers outside of your backyard, I can't think of a better tool than Google Hangouts.

Best Practice: Record Your Interviews

I love interviewing people using Google Hangouts. We will interview an expert in our industry or a client and use it as a case study.

These interviews get instantly published to our YouTube channel, and we are able to use them in our eNewsletters and on our social media platforms. To give it a try, go to http://www.google.com/+/learnmore/hangouts/onair.html.

SECTION SEVEN

Turn Your Customers into Your Sales Force

I'M SURE YOU HAVE figured out by now that I'm a big Dale Carnegie fan. Besides having many of its franchises as clients, I am also a graduate of all of the courses. After taking the original Dale Carnegie course, I wrote my vision statement, which became a roadmap for my first book. I took their sales course, and I learned how to express the value of my services without sounding like an aggressive salesperson. And if that wasn't enough, I also became a more powerful speaker by investing in its High Impact Presentations program. So yes, I'm a believer. I don't just drink the Kool-Aid, I bathe in it.

So why am I telling you this? Well, I believe your customers can be great salespeople for your business. I firmly believe I can sell Dale Carnegie training better than I can sell my own solutions. Why? Simple. In the eyes of the person with whom I'm speaking, I am not selling. I'm sharing my opinion with no benefit to me. Therefore, it's ten times more credible and effective.

Social media gives us a golden opportunity to allow our customers to sell for us.

So give your customers every opportunity to sell for you!

I hate cold calling. When I pick up the phone and have to explain the value of our company, I literally feel like I want to throw up in my mouth. I'm not good at it, and I find it to be a complete waste of time. I would much rather have someone else whom the prospect knows and trusts introduce us through a recommendation. There is nothing like a referral from a mutual acquaintance to immediately gain credibility.

On average, 14 percent of people trust advertisements. Eighty percent trust peer-to-peer recommendations (nielsen.com).

This is nothing new, of course. Almost every business will say that its primary marketing strategy is word-of-mouth. And, as my friend Erik Qualman says, social media is simply word-of-mouth on steroids. If you can get your raving fans to sell your products or services, you can pretty much do everything else wrong and still make the sale. That is how powerful an endorsement, positive review, or referral is in helping a buyer make a decision. The challenge is getting people to act. People tend to be much more motivated when they are unhappy than when they are happy. So we must be proactive in getting our champion customers to sell us to their friends, family, and colleagues. The following chapters will offer my favorite strategies for getting customers to sell for you. Let's begin!

17

GET POSITIVE REVIEWS ON THIRD-PARTY SITES

I WROTE ABOUT ONLINE reviews earlier in the book, but it is important to mention them here as part of letting your customers sell for you. People often look at third-party sites before making a buying decision. Sites like Google+ Local Business, Yelp.com, Kudzu.com, UrbanSpoon.com, and others allow users to write reviews about your business. Although some may disagree with me, I don't see any issue with you asking your customers to review you on some of these sites. I'm not suggesting you ask your sister or cousin to write a review; I'm suggesting that when someone is patting you on the back and sharing their positive experience, you should direct them to one of these sites for a review. Keep in mind that people are generally much more motivated to review a business when they're unhappy than when they're happy. I believe you need to be proactive in requesting reviews from your happy customers.

The first step is determining which third-party sites should have your attention. The easiest way to do this is by performing a few Google searches for critical keyword phrases in your industry and see which sites rank on the first few pages. For example, in the south, Kudzu.com is a very popular directory for many service businesses. They rank very high for searches like "bathroom remodel Montgomery, Alabama" or "tree service Alpharetta, Georgia." So, if you were in one of these industries and had locations in the south, then Kudzu.com might be a site where you would be proactive about getting reviews.

Some sites are stricter than others when it comes to owner-solicited reviews. Yelp.com attempts to filter out reviews it believes were solicited by the owner of the business. You will just have to work within the rules of each directory and do the best you can.

Once you have determined the sites where you need more reviews, then it is time to communicate with your customers about where you'd like them to write a review for your business.

Best Practice: Here Are a Few Ways to Request Reviews

- Send an email marketing piece
- Get your staff to ask their customers at the appropriate time
- Use social media sites like Facebook or Twitter
- Place an in-store sign in an obvious place

FAQ: Can I just get reviews from customers and post them myself?

Unfortunately, no. On sites like Google+ and LinkedIn, customers need to write the reviews themselves. At restaurants, I often see comment cards stuck inside with the bill. What are they going to do with that? Post it on a bulletin board in the kitchen? That's so old school! Instead, stick a card in there with instructions for how to leave feedback on your Google+ Local business page or UrbanSpoon.com!

FAQ: Can I incentivize my customers to write a positive review?

That is a really sticky question that I often have a tough time answering. On one hand, it seems as if you are bribing your customers. On the other, you may just want to thank them for taking the time to do something nice for you. I will leave this one up to your best judgment. With some things, the answer is simply whatever feels right to you.

Case Study

My friend Jamie owns a jewelry store in Roswell, Georgia. He prides himself on building relationships and not making customers feel like they are in a high-pressure sales situation. I recommended the store to another friend of mine looking for a small stocking stuffer for Christmas. After my friend left the store, this is the text message I received:

"Corey, thanks for sending me to Jamie. I came in with a very limited budget and not once did he ever make me feel unimportant. He now has a customer for life."

Wow. What a testimonial. The problem is, I'm the only one who got to see it. Luckily, Jamie is not just a friend—he's also a student! When I shared the message, Jamie immediately asked me to text my friend back and direct him to the store's Google+ Local business page to post the review. Once the student, now the teacher!

18

LET YOUR LINKEDIN PROFILE SELL FOR YOU

AT A RECENT SPEAKING event, I was in the back of the room waiting to go on stage. I was standing next to the meeting planner, and we were quietly chatting while the other speaker was wrapping up.

I asked her how she found me for the event and she quickly replied, "A LinkedIn recommendation."

"A single recommendation?" I asked.

"It was from the guy at Medical Solutions," she continued. "He said you spent time customizing your presentation and made it simple and interactive for his audience. That is all I needed to hear."

LinkedIn recommendations are a powerful way for people to learn about the value you provide. The key is getting the right recommendations. I strongly believe in quality over quantity. I would rather see six really strong recommendations than twenty-five weak ones. A strong recommendation is from someone who has purchased a product from you or used your services and had an amazing experience. When they write their recommendation, they will use language that will mean something to a potential buyer. They will talk about how you saved them money, made them money, or made their life better. On the flip side, a co-worker might talk about your energy, timeliness, great attitude, and things of that nature. That's okay, but probably not going to convince a prospect on why they should buy from you.

*Make sure your recommendations
are from champion customers.*

Take Action!

I want you to jump on your LinkedIn profile and request at least three recommendations from past or current customers. In order to do this, you will need to be connected with them on LinkedIn. When the box appears to write a note, take that opportunity to tell the person why you have chosen them for the recommendation. The more thought you put into this note, the more likely they will be willing to do it for you.

Best Practice: Give Them Some Input on What You Are Looking for in the Recommendation

If you have a good relationship with the person you're asking to recommend you, then you might help direct them in the type of recommendation you're looking for. After a presentation, I send a note to the meeting planner thanking them for all they did to put on such a great event. I also ask for a LinkedIn recommendation. In that note, I explain that other meeting planners will be the target audience, so please direct their words toward that audience. I might even share some questions for them to answer to get them started:

- How was my preparation before the event?
- Did I deliver the customized content you were looking for?
- Did I stay long enough to answer questions and interact with the audience?

I find that people generally appreciate this since it makes their job of writing a recommendation somewhat easier.

19

TURN A COLD CALL
INTO A WARM LEAD

WE HAVE COME TO my favorite strategy in all of social media. When I share this with an audience, I love watching their jaws drop to the floor. It's also the best example of how social media is truly changing the way we do business...forever.

As I mentioned earlier, I absolutely despise cold calling. Throughout my career, I have searched for better ways to sell. Before social media, I would do my best to help facilitate introductions from my best customers to decision makers with whom they had relationships. It was long and tedious work, but if I got the right two people together, it was magic. Once my customer was through gushing over us, all I had to do was not screw it up.

A few years later, I was playing around on LinkedIn before a meeting with a prospect. I decided to do some research by looking up his profile. While learning about his past experience, hobbies, and interests, I noticed the **number 2 next to his picture.** As I investigated this further, I realized it meant that I was connected to someone whom he was connected to. In this big ol' goofy world, we both knew the same person! But who was it? As I scrolled down a bit further, LinkedIn was kind enough to tell me exactly who this mutual connection was. It happened to be a client of ours who lived three states away. Never in my wildest dreams would I have known this mutual connection existed. I quickly called my client and asked him how he knew Steve (the prospect). It ended up that he knew him very well. My client sent one of those gushy emails to Steve 15 minutes before our meeting. The sale was made before I even entered the room.

In the old days (like in 2003), I would have somehow needed to figure out just at the right moment that my client knew Steve. This would have been impossible.

With LinkedIn, the power is not in your network. It is in your network's network.

Only connecting with the people you know is nothing new. In the old days, they called this a Rolodex! It's the way LinkedIn enables you to tap into other people's Rolodex that is the game changer.

Say you were tasked with opening a new account with a company. Before LinkedIn, you might have called the company and reached the dreaded gate-keeper. Good luck with that! They are experts in not letting you through to the decision maker. And even if you get to the decision maker, you are just another sales guy (or gal) taking up their precious time.

I've got a better idea.

Log in to your LinkedIn account and do a search for that company. Most companies have a profile and will tell you all kinds of valuable things about the organization. It will also list all of the employees that work there and have linked their personal account to the company page. In most cases, you will see a nice list of executives (or decision makers) at the company. You will also hopefully see that magic number 2 next to a few of their names. Simply click on those decision makers and look for your mutual connection. If it's someone who could easily give you a referral to the decision maker, the next step is to contact your mutual connection and see how well they know this person. On LinkedIn, this is called the "Get Introduced" feature, and you will see it when you're on the prospect's profile. You can use the feature to get connected to the prospect, or you can simply email or call your mutual connection and do it that way.

Now, if they tell you that they just recently met this person, then don't ask for the referral—it will do no good! But if they have a solid relationship, go for the introduction! You will have turned a cold call into a warm lead.

There are a couple of rules in this strategy that you need to follow. First, make sure you have a good working relationship with someone before you ask them to make an introduction for you. I've been on the other end of a request where I had to say no because I had never worked with the individual. It's best not to put people in an uncomfortable position. Also, if you call your mutual connection and they don't have a solid relationship with the decision maker you're trying to meet, the conversation should stop right there. The relationship needs to be strong between both you and the mutual connection as well as with the mutual connection and the decision maker.

If you apply this strategy consistently, the results can be powerful. And I will not object if you decide to send me a commission check after your first sale. Joking!

FAQ: Is there anything I need to do to my profile before trying this strategy?

This strategy will not work unless LinkedIn knows exactly who you know. In other words, you need to connect with all of the people who potentially could introduce you to new prospects. I recommend trying to get to at least

500 connections. I know this seems like a lot, but most people know 500 people. By simply spending some time on LinkedIn, you will quickly start to see people who you know but just forgot to connect with. You will be up to 500+ connections in no time. The higher the quality of these connections, the better the "Get Introduced" feature will work for you.

FAQ: Do I need a premium account on LinkedIn to use this strategy?

No, you can get started using the Get Introduced feature on LinkedIn using a free LinkedIn account. If you do this consistently, LinkedIn may limit your number of tries or the number of profiles you can see. If that starts to happen, it may be a good time to upgrade to a premium LinkedIn account. For more information on premium accounts, go to http://www.linkedin.com/static?key=welcome_premium

SECTION EIGHT

All-Star Lineup
of Guest Authors

OVER THE PAST FEW years, I have been lucky enough to meet and learn from some amazing people in the digital marketing industry. A few of them have been gracious enough to offer their expertise on some specific topics I wanted to include in this book. If you're nearing social media overload, then you should stop and come back when you are ready. But if you are even slightly curious if these other topics can be of value to you or your business, do yourself a favor and read on. You will be learning from a *New York Times* bestselling author, someone who has accumulated millions of YouTube views, and other masters of the digital marketing profession.

I am truly humbled that I get to include them in my book. Enjoy.

All-Star Lineup:

Chapter 20 *Erik Qualman -*
YouTube Can Make You a Video Star!

Chapter 21 *Jay Baer -*
Twitter: The New Telephone

Chapter 22 *Terry Brock -*
Using Klout for Business

Chapter 23 *Michael Tigue -*
FAQs About Websites Answered by a Web Designer

Chapter 24 *Heather Lutze -*
Social Media & Search: A Marriage Made In Search Heaven!

Chapter 25 *David Newman -*
The (Real) IDIOT'S Guide to Social Media Marketing

20

YOUTUBE CAN MAKE YOU A VIDEO STAR!

By Erik Qualman

YOUTUBE IS THE SECOND largest search engine in the world. The explosion of mobile is also increasing the power and omnipresence of video. More than 100 hours of video are uploaded to YouTube every minute. This is a global phenomenon—80 percent of viewers are outside the United States. I learned first-hand how powerful YouTube can be for a business. Because of loyal viewers, my social media video series is the most watched of its kind in the world. The first video, "Social Media Revolution," is the one that truly changed the game for me (https://www.youtube.com/watch?v=sIFYPQjYhv8). Since then, I've been able to fail, learn, and succeed over the years with online video and you can, too.

One of the top questions I receive after giving a keynote speech on digital trends, reputation, or leadership is: "How can we make a viral video?" But that, you see, is the wrong question to ask. If you go into video production with the end goal of making a viral video, you are certain to fail. The correct question is always: **"What kind of video can we produce that will provide value to the viewer?"** The viewer makes things go viral, not you, the producer. There are some things we can do as producers to help give our videos a chance to go viral, which I discuss in this chapter, but you always must start with the viewer in mind. Again, when it comes to our digital world, we always need to think outward looking in, rather than our historic *Mad Men* approach of inward looking out.

Another question I am often asked is: "What compelled you to make the first 'Social Media Revolution' video?" The reason I produced the first video was simply as a tool to help explain social media, especially to small business owners and executives who weren't digital natives. As laughable as it seems now, not everyone really understood the power of social media. This was at a time when MySpace (remember it?) was bigger than Facebook. Many brushed off social media as simply being "something that teenagers do." In short, I was having a difficult time convincing people that social media was the next big thing for everyone. So I decided to do two things: write the first edition of my bestselling book *Socialnomics* and produce a complementary video.

I'd seen a great video called "Shift Happens," produced by Karl Fisch and Scott McLeod, on changes in education. I decided that I needed to make something like this, but completely centered on social media. I've produced many videos since then, and even own my own production arm (Equalman Productions)—developing videos for some of the top brands in the world. Disney has even come calling.

What follows are some key insights. I put the first video on a YouTube channel labeled Socialnomics09 rather than Socialnomics. The reason was that I wanted to test to see if it would work properly before putting it onto my main YouTube channel. Well, did it work! I received hundreds of thousands of views in days. The problem this created was that I needed to keep it on this channel (Socialnomics09). YouTube will not allow you to move videos and their views to another channel—the number of views will start at zero rather than at 200,000. Hence, I've been stuck with putting all my videos on Socialnomics09. I've since discovered that this has happened to many people I know. So, my first piece of advice is to test everything on your main channel because viral can truly happen overnight and you don't want to be pinned to a test channel.

"Going viral" is not a strategy. However, here are five key steps you can take to give your videos a chance at going viral:

Good music: Unless your video is of a cute baby or an extraordinary kitten, the music you select will be critical to its success. In various countries, YouTube's Content ID program allows you to use copyrighted music. As a *quid pro quo*, a pop-up window will display during your video listing the song title and artist and allowing users to click through to purchase the song. YouTube and the music label then share the revenue from the sale.

My advice is to find successful viral videos that are similar to the one you want to produce and determine what music they are using. You may seriously consider using the same music, as it has proven to be successful and the music owner isn't blocking it.

Keep in mind that your idea will not be new—as of the writing of this book, there are forty-eight hours of video being uploaded to YouTube every minute. Review videos similar to what you want to do and take note of what is and isn't working.

Note: YouTube's Content ID program can be a bit frustrating, since music labels and musicians often change their minds on when and where their music can be used. Hence, you may have three videos that use the same music and they all have 4 million views. Then one day, one of them has an error message saying the music is owned by EMI. Also, they may not work in every country. If you truly want to play it safe, either go through the steps of obtaining the rights or, for most, use royalty-free music.

Short and sweet: Definitely keep your video to less than five minutes, preferably a minute or less. In *Enchantment*, author Guy Kawasaki displayed data from research firm Visible Measures showing that 19.4 percent of viewers abandoned a video within the first ten seconds, and by sixty seconds, 44 percent had stopped watching. Lead with your most eye-popping content to gain and hold viewer attention. Don't build to a crescendo that may never be viewed.

Viewer is king: Only viewers make videos go viral. Yet often we produce videos from the vantage point of what we want to get out of them. This approach is wrong. We need to constantly ask: Am I providing something of value for viewers? What do they want to get out of it? If you have to include your brand, then make the mention short and preferably, at the end of the video.

Other purpose: Don't produce a video simply hoping that it goes viral. Produce a video with a clear purpose in mind. For example, you may produce a video for your sales team so that they can use it when they present to the board. If it goes viral because you adhered to the first three suggestions, it's a bonus! If it doesn't go viral, no problem; it is still a great tool being used by your team.

Share: When people ask for your original file so they can use it in their presentations or for other purposes, share it. Sure, there will be a few who do so with malicious intent, but they will be in the minority. The majority will be adding distribution points and beacons for your great work. They may make the video into something cooler than you ever dreamed of as well. Also, understand that YouTube data shows that videos often require a tastemaker to provide the crucial tipping point. In a well-known TED talk, YouTube showcased several popular videos that were dormant for months until a tastemaker like Jimmy Kimmel blasted it out to his legion of followers.

Guided by these five maxims, I produced several videos explaining the power of social media. Viewers pushed these to go viral, becoming the world's most viewed social media videos. Remember that making a viral video is not a sound strategy—making a video that provides value to the viewer is.

Case Study: Grand Rapids Lip Dub
(by Matt Qualman)

Situation

After *Newsweek* wrote an article calling it a "dying city," the people and businesses of Grand Rapids, Michigan were in a strong state of disagreement. A trio of residents in this west Michigan city decided they would get the word out to the contrary, their town was flourishing.

Action

They took to the streets, literally. The storyboarded idea was to put together a "lip dub" video that showcased the beautiful downtown of Grand Rapids and its cultural multitude of enthusiastic citizens. They solicited local businesses for financial and resource support. They ended up with more than twenty sponsors of varying participation levels, covering the $40,000 production budget. The final video involved a shutdown of the downtown to Grand Rapids and roughly 5,000 people lip synching to a cover of Don McLean's "American Pie."

Result

The video went viral, reaching 4.2 million views on YouTube in the first four months, cracking the top ten for most viewed video in the world on 5/28/11.* To date, there are hundreds of thousands of Facebook likes/shares. In addition, the project received huge coverage across traditional media outlets and blogs, greatly increasing its message and reach.

A very conservative estimate would put the total media impressions at roughly 15 million to date, when you add in the video views, articles, social reach, and blogs. Utilizing an average cost per thousand (CPM) of $20, you could easily say they received roughly $300,000 worth of media impact on their $40,000 investment (15M*$20/1000 = $300,000). And keep in mind the final video is over nine minutes long, which is a lot of thirty-second commercials.

The global reach and impact of this campaign resulted in its creators—Jeffrey Barrett, Rob Bliss, and Scott Erickson—forming a new agency called Status Creative.

Link to final video: http://youtu.be/ZPjjZCO67WI

Key Learnings

Reach and exposure in social media can be achieved with much less investment than traditional media or Internet display ads.

Creative and entertaining executions are in demand by consumers and will be rewarded by being shared within the social sphere.

Community outreach can be powerful; there are masses of proud citizens who are willing to contribute for a town, a product, or an industry.

*http://www.facebook.com/GRLipDub?sk=info

Death of Instruction Manuals

Don't like to read instruction manuals? Then go on YouTube and watch video demonstrations explaining everything from how to activate the auto flash on your camera to building IKEA furniture. Unlike the manuals, these videos explain the most important things quickly and come across as more personal. The video assistance is particularly helpful for visual learners. This is more productive and enjoyable than leafing through an outdated fifty-page manual in three foreign languages that's difficult to comprehend. A written instruction manual will soon be a relic of the past.

You or your business will also become a relic if you don't embrace the power of YouTube. Do as I did to grow the success of my business when it comes to YouTube: fail fast, fail forward, and fail better. And remember, it's not about you, your company, or your brand; it's about the viewer. Viewers determine your success or failure, so be certain to develop your videos from the outside in instead of from the inside out.

Erik Qualman has been featured in media outlets from *60 Minutes* to *The Wall Street Journal* and used by organizations from the National Guard to NASA. His book *Digital Leader* propelled him to be voted the 2nd Most Likeable Author in the World behind Harry Potter's J.K. Rowling. His 2014 book *What Happens in Vegas Stays on YouTube* is being adopted by organizations across the globe.

21

TWITTER: THE NEW TELEPHONE

By Jay Baer

EVEN THOUGH FAR MORE people use Facebook every day, Twitter may have had the largest societal impact of any social network yet devised. That's because Twitter has become the global water cooler where everyone has an opinion and shares it freely.

Twitter has changed fundamentally in the past few years. Indeed, it was once the place to tell people what you were having for lunch (an oft-leveled criticism among non-users). But that's far less accurate today. Twitter is now less about self-absorption (unless you're in the Kanye West category), and more about news/information and instant reactions to that news/information. Twitter has become headline news for the mobile age, interwoven with a comments mechanism.

Here are the top seven Twitter mistakes that I see most often. Hopefully, by describing these errors or misconceptions, I can assist you in improving and optimizing your own use of this incredibly important technology.

The Top Seven Twitter Mistakes

Not understanding the dual nature of Twitter
Not adhering to the 5x1 rule
Not having an editorial calendar
Not tweeting enough
Being driven by media, not by social
Underutilizing images
Not testing and measuring

Not Understanding the Dual Nature of Twitter

Twitter—and especially Twitter used for a business—is actually two separate initiatives with differing objectives and outcomes. The first (and most important) is reactive Twitter, where you are using the social network to answer customer questions and solve problems. This is customer service on Twitter, and it's a MUST, as more and more consumers turn to social media in lieu of legacy connection options such as email and telephone.

The second part of Twitter is the more commonly understood element—proactive Twitter. This is where you tweet about what is interesting, important, humorous, and meaningful to you—and hopefully, to your followers as well.

Be very aware of this dual nature when you think about your use of Twitter and what it means to you and your business.

Not Adhering to the 5x1 Rule

It's often been said—and wisely so—that Twitter functions like a cocktail party. You may be acquainted with some of the participants, but many are strangers to you. And in an environment like that, it would be poor form (and conversationally ineffective) to burst into the room and immediately and incessantly tell people how fantastic you are.

The 5x1 rule saves you from that fate on Twitter. It's inspired by social media pioneer Chris Brogan, and dictates that for every tweet you send that is about you or your business, send at least five that are about someone or something else that has merit. This may sound counterintuitive, but I can promise you it's true. The more you shine the spotlight on other people on Twitter, the more that spotlight will eventually shine back on you.

Not Having an Editorial Calendar

Yes, if you find something interesting or funny or memorable, you may want to consider tweeting it. But those "in the moment" posts should be the exception, not the rule. Most of your weekly Twitter participation should be semi-planned, the same way a magazine is semi-planned.

Think about a weekly magazine like *Sports Illustrated.* When the editors finish this week's issue, they know they have to immediately start creating the next week's edition. They don't know precisely what will go into next week's magazine because sports news and other stories are still developing and playing out. But, they know that they will have one or two longer features. They know they will have a column in the back and the "Scorecard" and "Faces in the Crowd" sections up front, as well as other elements that occur in every issue.

You should be thinking about your proactive Twitter in the same way. Approximately how many tweets per week will you send about your business? How many about you and your personal life (which is usually far more interesting than anything else)? How many about your industry or your city? Will you tweet at night? On weekends?

Make an editorial calendar for your proactive tweeting (remember the 5x1 rule) and use it as a guide to your weekly participation.

Not Tweeting Enough

The truth is that most people don't tweet often enough. This is because they don't want to "bother" their followers and "barrage" them with too many tweets. This is misguided thinking, however, because the percentage of your followers that see any one tweet you send is quite small.

Twitter isn't like email where, if you send a message to someone, it stays in their inbox and they are quite likely to see it eventually. They may delete it, but they'll at least receive the message. On Twitter, there is no "inbox" per se. When you send a tweet, only the people that happen to be on Twitter at approximately the same time are likely to see your message. This is a fraction of your total followers.

Thus, I believe you should consider sending five or more proactive tweets per day, plus as many reactive tweets as are necessary to provide customer service. Spread those proactive tweets throughout the day, to reach different people who use Twitter at various time intervals.

Free tools like Buffer help a great deal with this, as they allow you to create multiple tweets at one time, and then send them every few hours at specific times of your choosing.

Being Driven by Media, Not by Social

Remember, the magic of Twitter is not its potential as a broadcast mechanism for your brilliance, but rather its potential as a connection mechanism for you personally.

If people comment on your tweets, or retweet you, or favorite your tweet, take the time to interact with them. Use Twitter lists (a massively important feature) to create various "lenses" that allow you to look at Twitter more specifically. I have a Twitter list of friends and a Twitter list of clients, for example. I use these to stay up-to-date on what a smaller, specific group of people are tweeting. This allows me to proactively interact and engage with them, when appropriate.

Also, take time each week to connect to people in your industry, city, et al, by following a new batch of Twitter users. Utilize a tool like Follower Wonk to find new people that may be of interest to you.

Underutilizing Images

Like most forms of social media, photographs are now a major part of the Twitter experience. Append photos to your tweets wherever relevant, and you'll see your results increase significantly. This is much easier to accomplish when you use Twitter from a mobile device, of course.

Not Testing and Measuring

Speaking of results, most people do not spend enough time looking at what works for them on Twitter and doing more of what works and less of what doesn't work.

I very much recommend using a tool like Buffer or Hootsuite (both have mobile apps, too) to send all of your tweets. Both tools have integrated statistics, meaning that you'll be able to look at your history of sent tweets and see how many clicks, retweets, replies, and favorites each tweet accrued. You'll also be able to see what time each tweet was sent, and on which day of the week. Combined, these data points give you a trove of insights into what type of tweets are most effective for you, and when. This should be used to modify your editorial calendar on a regular basis.

Best Practice:
Similar to a fitness regimen, to do Twitter well requires time and commitment. Each morning, set aside twenty minutes or so to craft proactive tweets based on your editorial calendar, and use Buffer or Hootsuite to release those tweets throughout the day. Then spend approximately five minutes every two to three hours interacting with followers, sending reactive tweets, sending "in the moment" tweets, and so on. Total time spent per weekday is approximately thirty-five to forty-five minutes.

Case Study

If you have a blog or other online content that you want to crow about on Twitter (remembering the 5x1 rule), it's a good idea to tweet about that content more than once. I have a "nights and weekends" component of my personal Twitter editorial calendar, where I send one tweet each night, and one per weekend day. These tweets contain links to "greatest hits" blog posts that I have written in the prior thirty to 180 days.

In 2013, that one minor addition to my editorial calendar generated 13,139 visits to my blog.

FAQ: Should I use hashtags in my tweets?

Hashtags (the topic descriptions that are denoted with a "#" sign, such as #SocialMedia) are an important part of Twitter, and increasingly in all social media because Facebook and Google+ have also incorporated them.

They are utilized to help Twitter users find and sort tweets about a theme. Thus, if you have a tweet that contains information about a theme or a trending topic, by all means, use it. Never use more than two hashtags, however. Also remember that hashtags count against your 140-character limit for tweet length.

Several free or inexpensive tools can help you find popular hashtags, even showing you hashtags for your own city or state. See TrendsMap.com or WhatTheTrend.com for assistance.

Jay Baer is a marketing keynote speaker, social media and content marketing consultant, and author of the *New York Times* bestseller *Youtility: Why Smart Marketing is About Help not Hype*. Jay's blog, Convince & Convert, was named the number one content marketing blog in the world by the Content Marketing Institute. He's also host of the popular Social Pros podcast. For more information, visit JayBaer.com.

22

USING KLOUT FOR BUSINESS SUCCESS

By Terry L. Brock, MBA, CSP, CPAE

WHEN YOU TALK TO successful people in business about what helped them become successful, inevitably, somewhere in the conversation, they talk about relationships. Successful people know that establishing, building, and maintaining mutually beneficial relationships are most important for long-term business success.

This is the essence of social media and why it is so popular. Social media has turned the old method of advertising and marketing upside down. It used to be that brands would embrace the old "spray and pray" method. They would blast a message to anybody who might be out there—praying that someone, somewhere, somehow might hear what they are talking about and want to buy.

What a pathetic waste of resources!

What an annoyance to those who didn't want to hear the message!

Social media, when done right, focuses on engagement (key term!) with people in a mutually beneficial way. Social media connects human beings in a genuine, helpful way.

This is where the social measurement tool Klout comes into play. Klout is a social media measuring tool that lets you determine the amount of influence that someone has on a scale of zero to 100 (100 being the highest). If you're doing social media right, Klout will let you know with a higher score. Conversely, if you're not doing social media optimally, your Klout score will decrease.

Using Klout is a great way for businesses to reach their most enthusiastic customers and deploy what we call advocate marketing. Advocate marketing is best described as having someone else talk about how good you are. If I say I'm wonderful, you doubt it. If someone who you respect says I'm wonderful, you pay a lot more attention. Someone who is an advocate marketer will be more influential with others.

We've known about this important aspect of influence for many years. When someone is highly influential, people want them embracing their message and advocating for them. We have long seen celebrities endorse products for this very reason.

Klout uses a similar approach. However, instead of using very expensive celebrities, they use real people who are using the products and services of given brands and it generates much more enthusiasm.

Case Study

Chevrolet used Klout when it wanted to reach highly influential people with a love of the environment and of cars. Chevrolet gave these advocate marketers the use of a Chevy Volt for a long weekend. The influencers were not required to say anything good about the car. They didn't even have to say anything at all. The result was that many of these influencers raved about features they liked in the Chevy Volt. Those who were following these influencers became more interested and yes, this resulted in more sales for Chevrolet.

Case Study

American Airlines ran a promotion to reach more travelers by offering free use of its prestigious Admirals Club for a day to anyone who had a Klout score of fifty-five or higher. And no, they didn't have to fly American Airlines that day to get into the Admirals Club. Think about the benefits of travelers having a very positive experience in a new environment and then telling others about it through social media. That is effective advertising for American Airlines. It's good for the influencers who receive the perk. It's also good for those who read about it and think of trying the Admirals Club themselves.

Case Study

My friend J.B. Glossinger has a very successful podcast called Morning Coach. It has been rated as the number one podcast in the world for personal development. He discovered a wonderful way to benefit from Klout recently. He and his wife travel frequently between their homes in Ft. Lauderdale, Florida, and in Bogotá, Columbia. On a recent trip, they had to make a change in their schedule, coming back later than they had earlier anticipated. When he called the airline, he was informed that there would be an $800 change fee for the ticket.

Instead of just accepting that fee, J.B. recalled a conversation he had with me and my co-author, Gina Carr. We had told him about Klout and how many businesses are using it to market more effectively.

J.B. told the airline that they should check out his Klout score and his social media accounts. Within the hour, the airline called back and told him they would waive the fee as well as upgrade him and his wife to the front of the plane!

Yes, Klout matters! More and more businesses need an extra edge to find out who is active in social media and particularly who is very influential in given areas. Brands want highly influential people saying good things about them. This makes imminent business sense. With Klout, they are able to better allocate the resources for marketing and advertising by using word-of-mouth in a powerfully effective social media way.

Get to know what Klout is and how you can benefit from it in business. The perks will be of particular interest to you as businesses are actively seeking out highly influential people. You can check your Klout score by going to www. Klout.com. If you are on Twitter, you probably already have a Klout score. You might want to connect other social media networks that Klout counts like Facebook, LinkedIn, Google+, and others.

Let social media be a tool to connect you with important people. Let Klout be the tool to measure how effectively you're engaging with others on social media. Remember that business is really about building relationships and from those relationships you cultivate and build your bottom line. Klout can help you effectively engage in mutually beneficial relationships and boost your own bottom line in business!

Speaker Hall of Fame member Terry L. Brock helps organizations leverage technology like social media and mobile devices to connect with customers and increase productivity. He is the co-author of the McGraw-Hill book titled *Klout Matters: How to Engage Customers, Build Your Digital Influence—and Raise Your Klout Score For Success!* He is a past editor-in-chief for AT&T's largest business blog and previously was chief enterprise blogger for Skype.

He can be reached at www.TerryBrock.com or on Twitter - @TerryBrock

23

FAQS ABOUT WEBSITES ANSWERED BY A WEB DESIGNER

By Michael Tigue

MUCH OF THE WEB has changed since Corey wrote his first book, and websites are no exception. Devices are getting smaller and attention spans are getting shorter, so we must design our sites to meet these new requirements. Below is a checklist of things you'll want to consider when either designing or redesigning your site.

FAQ: Is your website mobile-ready?

How does your website look when viewed from a smartphone or tablet? Are parts of your website cut off? Does the user have to zoom in and out to navigate the website?

The original website solution for mobile devices was to create a second, mobile-friendly website that mobile users would see instead of your main website. This approach was a good immediate fix, but there were some downsides. The mobile site was often a second website requiring content to be updated in two areas. Also, some users were familiar with the desktop website and were confused when being forced to view the mobile website.

Fortunately, a better solution has evolved. As such, if you are building a new website or updating your current site, the easiest mobile-friendly solution is to select a "responsive" template.

Responsive websites respond to the size of the device screen. In fact, they do this "responding" in real time. Instead of dividing the page into pixels or tables, responsive sites divide the content into columns, each of which are coded to be a certain percentage of the screen size on large screens. On smaller screens, the columns are coded to stack on top of each other when they reach a minimum width in pixels. Three pictures that might appear in a row on a desktop screen will "respond" to a smaller screen size and file into a column instead of a row. Navigation bars will often migrate from a long row of buttons to a simple single drop down menu. As you study responsive templates, you'll be able to recognize them quite quickly. A good example of a responsive website is www.saratooga.com. Open it up on your desktop or laptop and adjust the browser window to watch the website "respond."

An easy way to upgrade to a responsive website is to select a responsive template. These responsive templates range from $15 to $75 and are well worth the major design improvement they provide. You can find them at www.themeforest.net and www.templatemonster.com. Your web developer can copy your existing content over to the new responsive template.

FAQ: What about using Adobe Flash on my mobile sites?

Adobe Flash videos and features will not play or appear on iPhones, iPads, or iPods. As such, it is important to remove these elements from your website and replace them with more universally friendly elements.

FAQ: Is your website compatible with social search?

Search engines are now placing more and more emphasis on whether people "like," "follow," or "plus one" your content. Therefore, you need to be creating relevant, new, and exciting content that other people can "like," "follow," and "plus." A few years ago, you received a big search ranking push by simply creating external content (Facebook, Blog, etc.) and linking to your website. Now, search engines are checking to see if real people are interacting and liking your content. If you think about it, this is a wise move on the part of the search engines. The human element makes it harder for you and others to fake popularity and relevance. As such, to earn those much needed extra page ranking points now, you'll need to actually provide popular content, promote the content, and offer the social media icons and links for visitors to show their favor.

FAQ: Is your website optimized for search engines?

Title tags are still very important and should contain your keywords, your company name, and your geographic location if it pertains to your type of business. Title tags should vary somewhat for each page on your website. For example:

Home Page - <title> Cherylyn Elite Color Hair Salon in Armonk & Westchester NY</title>

Stylists Page - <title>Elite Hair Color Stylists at Cherylyn Salon in Armonk & Westchester NY</title>

Notice how we kept all the main keywords but clearly described the stylist page.

The file name for a page should contain a relevant and descriptive word if possible, yet it should not be overly stacked with keywords. hair-stylists.html is a descriptive file name, but hair-stylists-in-armonk-new-york.html is too long. Also, you will annoy your web developer if you insist on long, confusing file names.

Header Tags (<h1>Our Elite Color Hair Stylists</h1>) are still important and are a great place to tactfully add keywords. Alternate tags for images are still a good idea, especially as image search increases in popularity.

Meta keyword and meta description tags provide less of a ranking boost than they did a few years ago. But the meta description tag is still often used as the descriptive text in a Google search result. Therefore, go ahead and keep them in place for now. Also, make sure your meta description tag accurately describes its page and does not contain the same text on each page. However, since you can't rely as heavily on meta tags, you'll have to continue to populate your website pages with relevant content, working in your keywords and phrases where tactfully possible. And, as previously noted, the more actively you can update and allow users to "like" your content, the more likely your site will be crawled by search engines.

FAQ: Will a visitor stay more than three seconds?

The World Wide Web as we know it is twenty years old. Users don't give every website they visit a long, thorough tour. If users find your site too hurtful on the eyes for any reason, they will likely bounce to another site in just a second or two. Therefore, your site must have the ability to retain visitors on appearance alone for a few seconds.

I am always amazed how many businesses have the absolutely most stunning furniture, woodwork, and showrooms, yet have absolutely disgusting websites. I am puzzled how the owners can understand so clearly the power of first impressions in person, yet neglect first impressions on the web. Don't make this mistake. If you wear nice clothes and comb your hair when you shake your prospects' hands in person, make sure your digital handshake is up to par as well. An old, ugly, messy website is equivalent to wearing old, ugly, messy clothing to a sales interview. You might be the best contractor for the job, but the prospect may never give you the time of day.

Take a good look at your website (read nothing), and consider whether your website provides a hurtful, neutral, or pleasing initial experience. If your website appearance is harmful, you need to update it immediately. Some industries and client bases can handle a website with a "neutral" appearance for now. But, as time ticks forward, only the best and most exciting websites will retain visitors beyond five seconds.

The Future of Website Design

The future may hold "pageless" websites. Well, to be fair, the website might be one long and interactive page. The idea of "pages" is a bit of a carryover from magazines and books. With new interactive coding abilities and the ease of finger swiping down, long, beautiful one page sites just may be the thing of the future. You probably don't need to worry about conforming to this approach just yet. But, it is something to keep in mind if you are due for a website makeover in a year or two. Also, consider the search optimization implications of ten pages of content tactfully placed all on one page.

————————————

Michael Tigue is the principal of Web4u Corporation, a website development and mobile app company in Atlanta, Georgia. Serving clients from major universities to law firms, churches, and even doggie day care centers, Web4u provides its clients with website and mobile app development and ongoing maintenance. Corey married one of Michael's high school classmates and met Michael at a class reunion in 2008. Corey keeps Michael up-to-date on the latest trends and ideas in digital marketing, and Michael uses his technological know how to implement Corey's concepts and solutions.

Michael Tigue
books@web4uonline.com
888-254-3213
www.web4uonline.com

24

SOCIAL MEDIA & SEARCH: A MARRIAGE MADE IN SEARCH HEAVEN!

By Heather Lutze

GRANDE, EXTRA HOT, SKINNY, non-fat, hazelnut latte with Splenda…

Why am I telling you my personal Starbucks coffee order? And what do individualized coffee orders have to do with keywords and social media?

People use both regular search engines and social media search engines to find exactly what they want, exactly the way they want it. They expect the results to be personalized to them, just like their Starbucks coffee order.

If I order a grande, extra hot, skinny, non-fat, hazelnut latte—and all I get is coffee, I am not going to be happy or satisfied. I will take my business elsewhere. Likewise, the "coffee" approach to marketing on Twitter, Facebook, YouTube, LinkedIn, etc., is not a strategy that will work for you. How do you make yourself "findable" on social media sites?

Simple—by strategically using keywords in everything you do. Yes, it will take some initial work, but you'll reap the benefits in a couple of different ways:

You'll be rewarded by your ranking in the search engines, because search engines are watching what's going on in social media. They're looking for key indicators to help them decide where to put you in search results.

If you use specific keyword phrases in your tweets, your blog post titles, YouTube video titles, in Facebook or LinkedIn profiles, then you are effectively conveying a message to Google about how you want to be found.

Just as when a customer gives her order to a Starbucks barista, and receives her perfect beverage, when a user puts her keyword phrase into the search box in Twitter or Facebook, she will receive the perfect result—you! By using the highly personalized keywords, and using them correctly, all of a sudden, you and the searcher are brought together. You're no longer just talking to yourself in a mirror; you are making warm, meaningful connections with prospects who have indicated an interest and you can show them how to come up with a solution…your product or your service.

Effective use of keyword phrases puts you in touch with a viable user audience that you can connect with, you can help, and last but not least—you can sell to.

"Social" search marketing is completely the opposite of traditional marketing techniques.

When you consider "findability," whether it be in pay per click (PPC), search engine optimization (SEO), or social media, instead of just hitting the biggest numbers, you need to be connecting with someone's Starbucks coffee order—meaning, their specific, detailed personal needs. It won't do you any good to try connecting with them via the word "coffee" or "chair." Because those searches lack intent and focus, they keep adding keywords to their searches to get better and better results. Bidding on a word like "coffee" or "chair" is a huge waste of time and resources, as is using them in social media content. How do you do that?

Some investigative work is required. You need to discover exactly how people search for your products and services. Really think about the consumer's path to purchase, including all the "informational, shopping, and purchasing" keywords.

Our job as marketers in social media—as well as in pay per click and SEO—is to really connect with our customers in a way that's meaningful to them, based on the keywords they just put into Google, or Facebook's search box, or search.twitter.com.

Using those main keywords in your Facebook wall posts, your tweets, the title of your video—is how you'll connect and get real value and bottom-line revenue for your business. When you think about social media marketing, think about the customer's process. Remember that it's your job to be found in ways that are meaningful to that customer.

If you want me as your customer, you have to speak to me. It's not enough anymore to speak to me as a coffee drinker; you have to speak to me with my own personal Starbucks order.

When you're starting to do your keyword research, you need to understand the buying cycle and focus on the shopping and purchasing keywords, the part of the process when people make buying decisions.

That's the point at which people join Facebook groups.

That's when they'll follow you on Twitter.

And that's when they're really interested in that subsection of whatever you have to offer that speaks exactly to their personal needs, their own individualized Starbucks coffee order.

FAQ: How do you choose your optimum keywords?

I recommend developing a list of thirty keywords. Here's the best possible place you can find these all important words—in the page search campaign or pay-per-click campaign you are already running. Simply pull the thirty or fifty top-performing keywords out of that campaign, and make a list.

If you already know your keywords from Google Analytics or another tracking tool that you have for your website, use them. Add your organic keywords to the list. These should be keyword phrases; two to three words in length are ideal for the shopping and purchasing part of the cycle.

One of my go-to tools is the Google AdWords Keyword Planner (Adwords.Google.com). This tool allows you to peek inside Google and see the number of searches for a particular keyword in the last thirty days, as well as an average of the last twelve months, both globally and locally. You will need to set up an account but you DO NOT need to enter a credit card. You can set up the account, skip the credit card info, and just use the Keyword Planner for your keyword phrase research

Size Up Yourself and the Competition

In the immortal words of Michael Corleone in *The Godfather Part II* (1974), written by Mario Puzo & Francis Ford Coppola: "My father taught me many things here… keep your friend close and your enemies closer." This is especially true of social media success. What brands and web sites do you see over and over? You are sick and tired of seeing the same competitors showing up when you don't. Let's do a bit of keyword espionage and see if we can learn some secrets about our competitors that we can leverage to our advantage.

Here is my spy toolkit:

SEMRush.com – An amazing site that allows you to enter your site as well as your competition to see exactly what keywords they are currently ranking for, what position they rank, and many other factors that will help you know your enemy.

WooRank.com – This site lets you to run a technical report on your competitors. See their social engagement or any technical issues from their site that is broken. Also, check your own site to see if you can tweak some issues and set up a keyword/social plan to eclipse your competitors.

CircleCount.com – Google+ is often the bastard step-child of the social media world. It is often held by business owners that it's Google's sad attempt to compete with sites like Facebook and Twitter. This is far from the truth. Google+ is an "identity platform." This social site helps Google to identify leaders in their field. It shows how fresh your thought leadership is in social marketing and is a direct connection to the latest update to Google's Algorithm, Hummingbird. Hummingbird establishes the authenticity of your expertise and thus impacts your website ranking. Google needs ways of establishing "authorship" on the Internet. Who is copying others' material and who is really the official author of that content? CircleCount.com will give you an idea of what your competitors are doing in Google+, how Google sees them as an expert, and what you can learn from their circle structure.

Don't forget to spy on yourself as well. See how these tools view your site, your site underbelly, and how you can reinforce your site and social presence to win the highest "authorship" in Google+ so that Google has no reason not to acknowledge you as a real deal expert and not a poser in your space.

FAQ: How do I make my content (blog or video) more searchable using social media?

The key to making sure your content is seen is by checking with the searcher using keyword research tools. You will discover what questions they are asking, what problems you can solve for them, etc. Secondly, make sure you use the keywords in what I call THBLI (Title, Headline, Body, Links, Images). Once you find your keyword phrase, create content that has the wording clearly spread throughout the asset, i.e., blog, Facebook post, yes, even a tweet. Remember, DO NOT spam content, just sprinkle it appropriately.

Remember, this content has to speak to robots and humans alike. Finally, share your thought leadership by starting with Google+ and then sharing it with other expert influencers in your space. Ask them to comment and share. Then make sure to take that one asset and set up a content calendar that redistributes it over multiple social media platforms so that you make the most of your time and energy to create the content. Now watch the results. A thought leader is someone who creates content on a continual basis, and keeps it fresh and current. Social media gives us the ideal platform to build our identity and thought leadership that finally proves to Google you deserve to rank and dominate search results. That is every business's social media end game.

Best Practice: Other Useful Tools

Google Hot Trends: (http://www.google.com/trends/hottrends)

Ads.YouTube.com/keyword_tool. This tool tells you what keywords people are using when searching for videos on YouTube, which can be a great resource if you're looking to title your videos.

Search.Twitter.com. This site will give you an idea of how people are searching and what keywords others are using in their tweets.

hashtags.org. This site shows you what hashtags are trending.

Heather Lutze is the widely acclaimed speaker, trainer, and consultant who literally wrote the book on search engine marketing. Two books, in fact—*The Findability Formula: The Easy, Non-Technical Approach to Search Engine Marketing* and the brand new *Thumbonomics: The Essential Business Roadmap for Social Media & Mobile Marketing.* Her writing and in-demand keynotes and workshops are delivered with the same witty, "no-geek-speak" style that has managed to demystify Internet marketing for countless business owners. For more info, go to www.findability.com.

25

THE (REAL) IDIOT'S GUIDE TO SOCIAL MEDIA MARKETING

By David Newman

TOO MANY BUSINESS OWNERS, marketers, and sales professionals want to get involved in social media but—sadly—do not understand the intent, ideas, or influence factors that could make social media such an effective tactic in their overall marketing arsenal.

How can I put this? Ummm...well, they're idiots.

Relax...IDIOTS is an acronym that stands for the six key misconceptions, faulty assumptions, and pillars of goofy thinking that prevent most thought-leading professionals (YOU perhaps?) from generating maximum results from your social media marketing efforts.

Let's explore these six mistakes and give you some strategies, pointers, and tactics to make sure you don't make the same mistakes.

I: "I, Me, My" syndrome

D: Dumb it down

I: Information without invitation

O: Over-selling

T: Talk without action

S: Short-term focus

Now, let's take a look at each of these six mistakes in a bit more detail—and how to do social media marketing the right way...

"I, Me, My" Syndrome

No, your social media postings do NOT need to be all about YOU.

In fact, if all you talk about is YOU—your company, your products, your services, your brand, your blog, your resources...people will ignore you, tune you out, and dismiss you for the self-centered IDIOT that you are. (Please remember IDIOT is an acronym—don't take it personally!)

How to do it right: Experts promote other experts. Experts are not insecure about shining the spotlight on others. Experts are curators and pointers out of cool things.

Experts invite other experts to post guest blogs on their websites (and they, in turn, get invited to do the same!). Experts share, collaborate, and cross-promote with other businesses with a genuine abundance mindset and not a scarcity mindset.

The mantra goes even beyond "give to get"—it is "give to give."

As long as YOU and YOUR COMPANY can be counted on to share interesting, relevant, valuable, sometimes even edgy content, guide your followers to the "good stuff" on-line, and position yourself as a reliable guide and sherpa in your area of expertise, you'll get PLENTY of attention, love, and respect, even MORE SO if you're not forever focused on hyping only yourself.

Grow up. Step up. Be a real expert and learn once and for all—it's not about YOU.

Question: When's the last time you promoted a fellow business owner, expert, or thought leader in any of your marketing communications?

Dumb It Down

This mistake comes from your fear that if you give away your VERY BEST ideas, strategies, tools, tactics, insights, and other secret sauce (yes, the very same ideas that go into your products and services—and with which you get paid BIG BUCKS from your paying clients!) that you will some-how diminish the demand for those same paid products and services.

So, you "dumb it down." You post that second-rate article. You remove some detail from that spec sheet because you want people to buy your consulting services and not do it themselves. You post the video that only has three of your ten key ideas because heck, if you gave all ten ideas, they'd never hire you—you've already "spilled the candy in the lobby."

Yep—you guessed it. That's IDIOT thinking rearing its ugly head!

How to do it right: The reality is—it works 180 degrees the other way. The ONLY way folks are going to pay you the big bucks is if they have a FIRST-HAND experience of your genius—if they feel it, taste it, touch it, and fully experience it. ONLY THEN will they want more. ONLY THEN will they share it with their colleagues. ONLY THEN will they call their boss over to look at your website or—better still—only then will they proactively email another decision maker your link.

Imagine if the Rolling Stones decided that they wanted to fill their concerts with fans paying $300 per seat for a stadium show so they could make tens of millions of dollars... and the way they pursued that goal is to forbid radio stations from playing their songs (gasp—letting people listen for FREE) and if they pulled their music from online sites like Amazon and iTunes because, gosh, if people can get the very same songs for ninety-nine cents, they would never pay $300 to come see it live.

When you put this scarcity thinking in the context of the music industry, you see exactly how ridiculously faulty this argument is!

Do you want to be SHARED—or do you want to be SCARED? Your call—but you already know which answer will make you more money. (Unless you're an IDIOT!)

Question: When's the last time you shared something for free that's so valuable, people have paid you good money for it in the course of doing business with you?

Information without Invitation

Social media sites and your blog are not a dumping ground for your second-rate press releases that you could never even get published in your local paper. Even rock-solid, current, highly relevant information is NECESSARY but NOT SUFFICIENT to fuel your thought leadership platform and build your empire as a smart company.

Here's a secret: the Internet actually does NOT need more information posted on it. Not from you. Not from me. Not from anyone.

How to do it right: An effective social media campaign will share information of stand-alone value and then INVITE a two-way (or five-way or 17-way) conversation around that information. How? Simple: ask questions, seek engagement, invite involvement.

EXAMPLES: On your blog, end each post with the following: "What do YOU think? Use the comments area below and share your experiences or advice on this topic." On Facebook, don't pontificate with your posts—engage your friends with questions such as: "How would you handle...," "Looking for good ideas on...," or "Just blogged about Topic X—would love to see a comment from you."

On Twitter, don't drop fortune cookie rants, ask QUESTIONS. Simple questions get amazing results, for example: "What's exciting in YOUR world?" "What are you working on right now?" or even have some fun with "fill-in-the-blank" tweets like: ""Fill in the blank: I'm passionate about _____." To further increase engagement on Twitter, feel free to SELECTIVELY add the request "Please Retweet" so your engagement question spreads even further. NOTE: Do NOT use this request on more than 5 percent of your tweets, otherwise you'll look sad, desperate, and lonely.

Offer value, seek opinions, spark conversation—and ask the most powerful question in sales AND marketing AND leadership AND relationships: "What do you think?"

Overselling

One particularly IDIOTIC business owner bragged proudly that ALL his social media posts have a hyperlink. Every. Single. One.

Hyperlink to where, you ask?

To HIS online store, HIS products, HIS consulting page, HIS services overview.

He said, "If you're not linking every post to a selling opportunity, you're just putting a lot of dead-end junk out there and you'll never make any money."

Now that is pure IDIOT thinking. And the sad news is that it's also the number one complaint that most buyers have about the way most business owners and small companies market themselves—namely, that it's all self-promotional hype with zero relevance to buyers or their organizations (and zero relevance to helping them solve their urgent, pervasive, expensive problems!).

Social media is not about posting "here's how to buy my crap". It's also not about creating an extra dozen or so sales pages for your products, services, or programs.

If your goals are: Sell on Twitter. Sell on Facebook. Sell on LinkedIn. Sell on YouTube...

Your results will be: Unfollow. Unfriend. Unlink. Unsubscribe. You're done. Buh-bye.

How to do it right: Content comes before commerce. Offer solutions, answers, strategies, templates, tools, and ideas—not sales messages.

Why? Because we're living in an environment of voluntary attention. The age of "old school" outbound selling (random cold calling, batch-and-blast direct mail, buying ads, and working hard to interrupt strangers) is broken.

The new reality is: First you earn their attention. THEN you earn their money.

Question: How can you turn your next sales message into a value message? How can you solve, fix, advise, and guide instead of hitting your prospects over the head with yet another blunt "buy my stuff" message? And which one do you think they will keep, share, forward, and remember you for?

Talk without Action

After just now discouraging you from overselling, the next mistake is leaving OUT a vital ingredient to your social media marketing efforts: a "Call To Action" (CTA).

Too many business owners, entrepreneurs, and independent professionals do almost everything right…but then leave their fans, followers, and subscribers wondering what to do next.

See how many of the following statements sound familiar:

"I've been blogging for two years and haven't gotten a single call or email about hiring me."

"I work for hours and hours on my ezine and although I get compliments about how good the articles are, I've never gotten business from it."

"I post all the time on Twitter, Facebook, and LinkedIn but I've never gotten a single phone call from any of my social media efforts."

How to do it right: The answer is simple—people need to be told what to do next. If you want people to email you, explicitly invite them to do so AND give them a compelling reason AND provide your email address. Example: My friend Scott Ginsberg always ends each blog post with an invitation similar to this one:

LET ME SUGGEST THIS...
For a list called, "9 Things Every Writer Needs to Do Every Day," send an email to me, and you win the list for free!

* * * *

Scott Ginsberg
That Guy with the Nametag
Author, Speaker, Publisher, Artist, Mentor
scott@hellomynameisscott.com

If you want people to call you, use the same strategy. Invite the call and provide your phone number. For example, Gerard Braud is a media training and crisis communications expert who introduces himself to hand-selected high-probability prospects on LinkedIn and ends his message this way:

If a brief conversation about your team's media-readiness and/or crisis communication plans would be valuable, please call me or drop me a line.
Wishing you continued success,
Gerard Braud (Jared Bro) Tel: 985-624-9976

Question: Are you using value-first CTAs in your emails, blogs, and social media postings? Are you giving people a compelling reason to engage further with you in meaningful ways such as subscribing to your ezine, calling you, or emailing you?

Short-Term Focus

The final mistake is to think of social media in the same way that you might think of outbound sales activity.

Think about it. Cold calls, email blasts, direct mail–do all these and the next natural question is how much did we sell today?

You made 100 dials, you connected with twenty humans, you had fourteen conversations, you qualified five serious prospects, and then how much did you SELL TODAY?

You sent 10,000 postcards. Requests came back for 300 quotes. So how many widgets did you SELL TODAY?

Social media marketing doesn't work that way. Social media is...well, social. It's about relationships and trust. Relationships and trust don't have an ON/OFF switch— they develop over time.

Transactions happen today from relationships you built last week, last month, and last year. The benefit of that— and the reason it's worth the "wait"—is that social media gives you a permanent asset: TRUST.

How to do it right: Blog entries are forever. They continue to sell your expertise, your company, and your value day after day, week after week, year after year. LinkedIn recommendations are forever. People who wrote glowingly of you in 2002 are still ""selling" for you and your reputation TODAY.

A voice mail? BEEP—gone. An email? ZAP—gone. A face-to-face meeting? DONE—bye. Those happen today, and they're gone today.

Sure, you have to sell today. You have to make your quota today. You have to feed your family today. But social media marketing helps you ensure that what you create ONCE today works and lasts and brings customers and clients to you for many years to come...

Not because you SOLD them like an IDIOT—but because you built the trust and relationships that HELPED THEM BUY today, tomorrow and beyond!

Question: What permanent assets are you building today so that your best-fit buyers will seek you out for your expertise, ideas, and solutions at the precise moment they are ready to spend money on what you sell? Are you putting irresistible bait on enough hooks in the right ponds so you won't go hungry next week, next month, and next year?

———————————

David Newman is a marketing expert, professional speaker, and founder of Do It! Marketing, a marketing strategy firm dedicated to making thought-leading entrepreneurs and executives more successful. David's book, *Do It! Marketing: 77 Instant-Action Ideas to Boost Sales, Maximize Profits, and Crush Your Competition* is available now. For marketing keynotes, seminars, and one-on-one consulting, contact David directly at david@doitmarketing.com or call (610) 716-5984.

SECTION NINE

Do or Do Not. There Is No Try

WHAT'S A TECHNOLOGY BOOK without a Yoda quote? These last few chapters are rules that you must follow in order to have success with the strategies in this book. Take them very seriously, as I have seen social media strategies flop because one or more of these rules were broken.

26

DO...HAVE
CONSISTENT MEETINGS

ONE OF MY FAVORITE coffee shops is Caribou Coffee. In fact, I wrote my first book, *eBoot Camp!,* during a Michigan winter in a toasty Caribou. You can imagine my disappointment when they decided to close a bunch of their stores around the country—including the one where my book was born.

But, this is not about my Turtle Mocha addiction; it's about the way Caribou Coffee handled the news about their store closings on social media. There was an avalanche of questions and concerns from customers on their Facebook business page. Instead of addressing them head on, the person (or persons) in charge of the page chose to ignore them and continue posting topics about coffee as if none of this was happening. Bad idea. This just enraged people even more and it snowballed into a PR nightmare.

I believe this could have been avoided if the company was having consistent meetings about their social media marketing. The topic of store closings could have been addressed and a strategy could have been created to address concerns and negative feedback. I even thought they could have invited devoted customers to come to Caribou stores that were closing and get a piece of merchandise for posterity's sake. This could have helped steer the angry mob toward their favor, but no such move was made.

So what can you learn from this? Most social media snafus could have been avoided with consistent meetings. If you plan to have an ongoing social media strategy for your business, then you should also have ongoing meetings. These can be monthly or even quarterly meetings, but all major shareholders of the business should be in attendance. **To be clear, you don't need to write every Tweet or post every Facebook message yourself, but if it is your company or you have an executive role at your organization, you must be involved in the planning.**

You need to know where the social media ship is going so it does not hit the proverbial iceberg.

Topics that could be covered during these meetings:

- **Upcoming Events:** What's upcoming and what needs to be promoted?
- **Social media team schedule**: Are there any planned vacations and who can step in for content?

- **Issues:** What happened over the past month (either to the business or to another business) and what can we learn from it?
- **Results:** How are we doing toward achieving our goals for the year? Which sites are working? Not working?
- **Brainstorming:** Need more fans on your Facebook page? Brainstorm a cool Facebook contest you can run. Struggling with content ideas? Ask the team to brainstorm a list of topics your followers will find interesting.

Consistent meetings help everyone stay motivated and on the right track. They also helps keep executives of the company involved in the overall social media strategy. Without these meetings, executives can get disconnected and therefore question the value of the entire initiative.

Best Practice: Beware of Automated Posts to your Social Media Sites

I facilitated a recent meeting at a fairly large company in California. During the "issues" section, an employee shared a story about a major gaffe that occurred on the day of the Boston Marathon bombings. A business seemed to have its social media posts pre-populated and had them sent out every hour. One of the posts referred to its product as being "the bomb" and was looked at as being quite insensitive in light of what had transpired earlier in the day. The employee mentioned that had someone been physically posting each of these, they probably would have not made that bad judgment call. It was a good reminder for the organization that in times of crisis, it is important that any post that goes out be focused on the crisis at hand and nothing promotional.

Best Practice: Calling All Business Owners and Executives

In my ten-plus years of doing Internet marketing and social media for companies, I have been a part of a lot of great success stories. But I have been a part of some failures, too. One consistent theme that has run through all of those failures is a lack of involvement from management. Now, that is not putting blame on the other foot as, in some cases, we needed to do a better job of keeping management involved. The point is that when management is oblivious to what is happening with their digital marketing, it is doomed to fail.

Get involved. Stay involved. Know what is happening—both positive and negative. The more involved you are, the better chance you will have to succeed.

27

DO NOT...
AGGRESSIVELY SELL

EVERYTHING WE'VE TALKED ABOUT in the book has one thing in common: **marketing**. You have to resist the urge to treat these tools like advertising strategies. Think of it like a gigantic conference. If you have a Facebook page, a LinkedIn profile, or a blog, you are simply attending the conference. Yes, there is business to be done, but you have to let it happen organically—you can't force it! If you walk up to someone and start promoting your products and services, you might as well have on a long trench coat with a variety of watches for sale.

FAQ: What if I paid for a Facebook or a Google ad? Should I still not sell in those cases?

Now that is a different story. That's like paying for a booth at the conference. People expect that you will be handing out flyers and sharing details about your company. You have paid for the right to be in advertising mode.

But, if your strategy is predominantly content marketing (blog, YouTube, email) and community engagement (Facebook, LinkedIn, Twitter), then you have to level your expectations a bit.

Add value first, add value second, and add value third.

Case Study

I remember when we first got to Michigan; I posted on Facebook looking for a dentist recommendation. A friend sent me a link to a website, which had a report on the five things coffee drinkers can do to keep their teeth white. I bit! For the next six months, I received quality articles about keeping my teeth clean and my body healthy. It was all value, no selling. I found them in January, and I became a customer in July. But they were able to stay Top of Mind until I was ready. Had they started blasting me with ads in January, February, or March, I would have opted out immediately.

Case Study

One of the most successful social media posts we created for one of our Dale Carnegie franchises was a big arrow that pointed to a person's profile picture that read, "I'm a Dale Carnegie Graduate." It started as a picture we post-ed on their Facebook company page, but quickly spread to many of Carnegies' graduate profiles. People started asking these graduates about Dale Carnegie and what it was all about. Give a Dale Carnegie graduate a chance to talk about their experience and be prepared for a love fest. There's a reason they have been around for more than 100 years. So people started selling their friends on the value of Dale Carnegie training without any involvement from the company itself.

When we share our value, it is selling; when our customers share our value, it is honesty.

Best Practice: Additional Tips to Keep You from Falling into the Dreaded Salesperson Trap

- Let others sell for you.
- Give people the opportunity to comment on your

pages. Remember, when they say it, they're not selling, they're telling.

- Find creative ways to get them from social media to your sweet spot. Think Free, think Fun, think… Fudge? I could not think of a third "F."
- Help people. Become a valuable resource to them.
- Make it about them. More on that in a minute….

28

DO...MAKE IT ABOUT THEM

PUT A STAR BY IT, circle it, write it on a sticky note, and paste it on your forehead. If you remember nothing else from this book, just focus on making it about them: the customer. Two Super Bowl Sundays ago, I posted what I considered to be the best social media advice I had ever given on my Facebook business page. It garnered two likes and one share. I was heartbroken. What was wrong with my fans? How could they not go share-crazy with this pearl of wisdom? A year later, I decided to offer a free copy of my book to the fan who came closest to guessing the score of the Super Bowl. It received 145 likes and twenty-five shares. I learned a valuable lesson that day: it's not about me or what I think is valuable. On Super Bowl Sunday, people are interested in…well…the Super Bowl!

So whether it is your social media postings, blog articles, or email marketing pieces, try to put yourself in the minds of your readers and figure out what they would find valuable. Our agency manages the social media marketing for forty-plus businesses, and we have a list of categories that rank high on the priority list of their fans. Here are some of them (in no particular order):

- The weather
- Sports teams
- Local events
- Holidays
- Inspirational quotes
- Accolades for city or state (example: lowest unemployment rate)
- Humor

Notice not one of these categories has anything to do with the business itself. That doesn't mean that you never talk about your business or promote your sweet spot; you earn the right to soft promotion between offerings of value.

Value, value, value, soft promotion, value, value, value, soft promotion…

Best Practice: The 75/25 Rule

Our team creates email marketing pieces for a kitchen and bath company. In our emails, we use 75 percent of the content to offer value to the readers and 25 percent to softly promote an offer from the company. We offer value by including articles that help educate the consumer on kitchen- and bath-related topics. These emails get double the open-rate (amount of times the email is opened) than any of their traditional, purely promotional emails. We offer value first, value second, value third, and then we sell.

FAQ: Is it okay to post articles I didn't write but think others would find interesting?

Absolutely! One of the ways to add value to your network is to be a curator of content for them. Because you are so involved in your industry, you come across valuable information every day. You can sort through that information and syndicate the content you find worth reading. That saves your network time and the more they enjoy your postings, the more they will trust your judgement and watch for content you post in the future.

Just make sure you do it the right way by linking out to the article so the author gets proper credit and the link juice. For example, if you thought this article from my blog was valuable enough to share with your network, you might post it like this:

Have you ever used the site zerys.com? Check out this article from my friend Corey on how to leverage the site for blog content: http://ebootcamp.com/blog/2013/08/26/the-importance-of-leverage/

Make it about them.

29

DO...START NOW!

THAT'S IT...WHAT ARE you still doing here? Go, get out of here, and get going!

You have everything you need to put your social media strategy in place and start seeing results.

Use this social media sales process: figure out how you will generate leads, build credibility, stay Top of Mind, lead people to your sweet spot, and turn them into happy customers.

SOCIAL MEDIA SALES FUNNEL

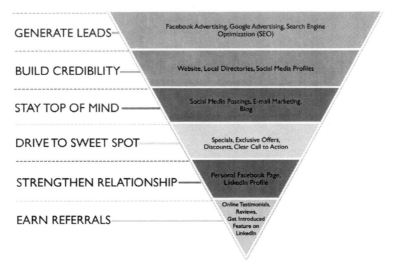

GENERATE LEADS — Facebook Advertising, Google Advertising, Search Engine Optimization (SEO)

BUILD CREDIBILITY — Website, Local Directories, Social Media Profiles

STAY TOP OF MIND — Social Media Postings, E-mail Marketing, Blog

DRIVE TO SWEET SPOT — Specials, Exclusive Offers, Discounts, Clear Call to Action

STRENGTHEN RELATIONSHIP — Personal Facebook Page, LinkedIn Profile

EARN REFERRALS — Online Testimonials, Reviews, Get Introduced Feature on LinkedIn

1. Pick the digital sites that are right for your business. This includes channels like email marketing, blogging, video marketing, etc.
2. Decide who is going to implement updates and manage the sites. Do you have the necessary resources internally? If not, don't let that stop you. Go out and hire good people (like us!) to do it for you.
3. Make sure you are using each of these sites correctly. Review the best practices and have consistent meetings to discuss your progress and goals.
4. Make changes, if needed. Not everything is going to work. Watch for lackluster results and make changes until you start to get some traction.

You have to figure this out. If you don't, you'll either keep trudging along without any significant growth, or you will be left behind by your competition.

I'll leave you with one final story. It is the story of a company that decided this was the year they would figure out the social media riddle. They sat with their team and created a plan. They focused on a few areas on the web where they wanted to do extremely well. They helped people by adding value wherever they could. They were proud of the communities they had created. They figured out exactly where their sweet spot was and, when appropriate, they drove people directly to it. Many of those people became new customers. They treated those new customers so well that those customers became their advocates and gushed over them on social media and review sites. It was a great year because you (I mean, they) decided to focus on a few and ignore the rest.

I sincerely hope this becomes your story for next year and for many years after. Go out and make me proud!

FAQ: What about syndicating my Twitter feed on my website?

Really?!!?

About the Author

Corey Perlman is a speaker, consultant, and nationally-recognized social media expert. His first book, *eBoot Camp!*, quickly became a bestseller and an international success. Corey crosses the globe speaking to companies and associations on how to generate real results from their social media marketing initiatives. He's spoken for companies such as Sysco Foods, Dale Carnegie Training and KTM-Sportmotorcycles. His company, eBoot Camp Inc., employs a team of highly-skilled digital specialists who manage the social media accounts of over 40 companies. When not working, this self-proclaimed, certified propeller-head enjoys long walks with his wife through the aisles of Best Buy and loves taking his two young children on summer vacations to Silicon Valley.

CPSIA information can be obtained at www.ICGtesting.com
Printed in the USA
BVOW05s0550280414

351789BV00005B/23/P